INSPIRATIONAL
INVESTING

INSPIRATIONAL INVESTING

What matters in the world of
investing – by women, for women

Edited by
AMANDA TAYLOR

Harriman
House

HARRIMAN HOUSE LTD
3 Viceroy Court
Bedford Road
Petersfield
Hampshire
GU32 3LJ
GREAT BRITAIN
Tel: +44 (0)1730 233870

Email: enquiries@harriman-house.com
Website: harriman.house

First published in 2022.
Copyright © Harriman House Ltd.

The right of the authors to be identified as the Authors has been asserted in accordance with the Copyright, Design and Patents Act 1988.

Paperback ISBN: 978-0-85719-962-1
eBook ISBN: 978-0-85719-963-8

British Library Cataloguing in Publication Data
A CIP catalogue record for this book can be obtained from the British Library.

CONTENTS

Foreword   VII

Introduction   1

Acknowledgements   5

Part 1: Women Are Different   7

Investing: When Should We Start Owning It?   9
Iona Bain

The Behavioural Science of Investing: What Can We Learn from   17
Gender Differences?
April Vellacott

Gender and Financial Risk Taking   27
Dr Ylva Baeckström

Part 2: Investment Planning   43

Financial Advice: What Are the Options and What Does It Cost?   45
Holly Mackay

How to Spot a Good Financial Adviser: An Adviser's Point of View   53
Lisa Conway-Hughes

Making Your Plan: An Investing Checklist   57
Becky O'Connor

Part 3: Money Stories   61

In Search of Gender Balance in Finance   63
Q&A with Baroness Morrissey DBE

Diversity: an Algorithm for Success?   71
Q&A with Julia Angeles, Marina Record and Rose Nguyen

The Value of ESG Investments   87
Q&A with Maria Nazarova-Doyle

Minding the Pensions Gap   103
Q&A with Jackie Leiper

Financial Literacy and Inclusion   113
Q&A with Claer Barrett

Diversifying your Portfolio with Investment Trusts   117
Q&A with Claire Dwyer

Making Money Mainstream   125
Q&A with Kalpana Fitzpatrick

Closing the Ethnicity Investment Gap   133
Q&A with Selina Flavius

The Financial Education Revolution   139
Q&A with Vivi Friedgut

Breaking Down Barriers in Investing   147
Q&A with Prerna Khemlani

Improving Financial Wellbeing   151
Q&A with Laura Pomfret

Disrupting Wealth Management   157
Q&A with Charlotte Ransom

Part 4: Useful Resources   163

Connect with other Investors   164

Resources Directory   167

A–Z of Investing   173

Partners   177

FOREWORD

As a financial journalist, statistics, numbers and charts cross my desk every working day. They include share prices, stock market indices, dividend yields, percentage rises and falls and many more besides. They are essential to doing my job but while this little parade of numbers is always varied and wide-ranging, it is rare for any one of them to stop me in my tracks.

Then one day, one number did. It was dropped into a conversation I was having with Jane Portas, co-founder of Insuring Women's Futures and author of *Living a financially resilient life in the UK*. What was the shocking statistic that made me draw my breath? It was this: by the age of 65 in the UK the average woman's pension will be worth one fifth the value of a man's.

Whatever your gender, it is impossible to dispute that this is anything other than calamitous and unacceptable. I have since heard the gender comparison presented in many different ways – some less grim than the one above – but no matter how it is calculated, each one reveals the same thing: men and women make starkly different financial journeys throughout their lives.

What shocked me too was the fact that I did not know, until that moment, quite *how* different financial outcomes could be if you were a woman. I was aware that women suffered from the gender pay gap, and that we were less likely than men to become private investors. I was not aware however how the roles that society has imposed on women would punish them financially – and severely at that – throughout their whole life.

But depressing as the gender wealth gap is, exposing it has done some good. It has sparked off a determination to prevent the same thing happening to new generations of women. It has made financial services providers, government departments, newspapers, magazine and book publishers, and many exasperated women sit up and take note, and to try to solve the problem. It has unleashed a chorus of voices unwilling to allow this built-in bias with deep foundations to continue. Remember, until quite recently the damage done to women's finances through no fault of their own was pretty much hidden from view from everyone.

Many of the reasons behind this gap are explored in the essays and interviews in this book. Some of them are obvious, such as women being far more likely than men to have jobs that pay low salaries leaving them with smaller amounts available to save in the first place, and the fact that they often exit the workforce for years – or permanently – when children come along and when elderly parents need support. Another factor which both April Vellacott and Dr Ylva Baeckström explore is that women have tended to be excluded from the 'male world' of investing. The idea that women are not investors has become entrenched, and then internalised by women. This lack of confidence and of role models compounds the problem. If we do not see our female relatives and friends investing, planning their finances, and discussing choices and strategies, then investing will remain out of reach, invisible and on the periphery. We will not learn that it is something we have to do – and we must, because no one else is going to take care of our financial future.

This book is an important new voice encouraging women to invest, to make it a normal and everyday activity for women. Investing isn't something to be feared. It means that you can make your money grow, that you can provide for your future self and remove the risk of depending on someone else to do this. You don't need to chase high risk, speculative assets to make money in the markets, nor are you required to be a Warren Buffett-style genius at stock picking. You can use index tracking funds and investment trusts as several of the contributors outline, and you can protect yourself by diversifying and staying invested for as long as possible.

These brilliant and insightful essays illuminate the risks of doing nothing. They will open your eyes to barriers that you may not even know exist and how you can surmount them. Every section is packed full of useful tips, guidance and sources to get you started.

I hope *Inspirational Investing* will inspire many of you to begin a new and more rewarding path to your future. If you lack female investor role models, you won't find better than the ones included in this book.

Rosie Carr
Editor, *Investors' Chronicle*

INTRODUCTION

"The success of every woman should be an inspiration to the rest."

Serena Williams

To start things off, it feels appropriate to address the idea behind this book. Through my work at Master Investor I've been very fortunate to meet many successful investors who have inspired my investing, many of whom are women. But I very much stumbled into my role in this industry and had I not, I may never have discovered these role models or learnt what I have along the way. The reality is that the majority of people just don't have exposure to the resources that are out there to support them with their finances, nor do they know where to begin looking for them. This is a key factor in why financial literacy is such a blind spot for many and, being truthful, our finances aren't the sexiest of topics to spend our spare time learning about, so most people just don't.

I have been supporting the International Women's Day movement for a number of years – the activities and campaigns are important for raising awareness of the challenges faced by women in their careers and personal lives. Finance is a key area where we see many gender gaps in pay, pensions and investing – the list goes on. Last year's International Women's Day theme was *Choose to Challenge* and the 2022 theme is *Break the Bias*. By choosing to read this book you have chosen to challenge, and I hope we encourage you to go out and break the bias.

As individuals and as a collective, we have the ability to break the bias in our communities, workplaces, schools, universities and personal lives.

Inspirational Investing explores the reasons why fewer women are engaged in investing for their future, the fight for equality and diversity in the financial services industry, the still-unresolved gender gaps in finance from pay to pensions, and why now is the time for more women to take investing seriously.

We start with some background on the behavioural differences between the genders when it comes to investing and our attitudes towards risk. We look at why it's important to take control of our money and why there's no time like the present when it comes to investing. Part 2 focuses on planning and the role of financial advice in our decision making. The third and largest part of the book comprises a series of interviews touching on a number of themes, from diversity in fund management through to impact investing and tackling pay and pension gaps. The final section has links to some resources you might find useful and an A–Z glossary of investment terms – we've tried to avoid jargon in this book but hopefully it helps with terminology you might spot elsewhere.

As you will learn from the following pages, we're well on our way to more balance, with more women taking control of their financial destiny, but a big shift is still needed and every person reading this book can be part of this change. Although it's very much a case that the system isn't perfect, the responsibility for continued change lies with us as individuals. If we reject the narrative that has been constructed and change our habits and behaviours with regard to our personal finances, the system will have to change to accommodate.

Thank you for choosing to read this book – *you* are where this change starts: *choose to challenge.* I hope you will find inspiration in these pages and that they will provide food for thought on your journey as an investor. Please do consider sharing what you learn with others, and of course through the kind support of our partners we are able to provide the ebook free of charge, so do share this far and wide to spread the word. ◈

Amanda Taylor

🐦 @AMANDAINVESTS

✈ @AMANDATM

⬀ MASTERINVESTOR.
CO.UK,
INVESTOLOGY.
ORG

AMANDA TAYLOR *is chief commercial officer at Master Investor, a financial media company and organiser of the UK's leading private investor event, the Master Investor Show. Amanda is also founder of Investology, a free newsletter that connects investors and rewards them for improving their investment knowledge.*

ACKNOWLEDGEMENTS

T hanks to everyone who has played a role in bringing *Inspirational Investing* to fruition. Without your help and support this book wouldn't be here to inspire readers to take the first or next step on their investing journey.

Special thanks to Harriman House for giving the project the go-ahead and allowing me to collate and edit the book. I appreciate you taking a chance on me as a first time editor/author and guiding me through the process of building a book. Special thanks to Sally Tickner, Myles Hunt, Tracy Bundey, Lucy Vincent and Nick Fletcher but also to the wider team – I know I haven't been in contact with many of you, but I appreciate all your hard work behind the scenes.

To our contributors, a big thank you for hearing our vision for the book and contributing your time and expertise:

Julia Angeles (Baillie Gifford), Iona Bain (Young Money Blog), Claer Barrett (*FT*), Dr Ylva Baeckström (King's Business School), Rosie Carr (Investor's Chronicle), Claire Dwyer (Fidelity), Kalpana Fitzpatrick (The Money Edit), Selina Flavius (Black Girl Finance), Vivi Friedgut (Blackbullion), Prerna Khemlani (This Girl Invests), Jackie Leiper (Scottish Widows), Baroness Helena Morrissey, Maria Nazarova-Doyle (Scottish Widows), Rose Nguyen (Baillie Gifford), Rebecca O'Connor (Good with Money), Laura Pomfret (Financielle), Charlotte Ransom (Netwealth), Marina Record (Baillie Gifford), April Vellacott.

To our publishing partners, Scottish Widows and Baillie Gifford, thank you for your support to enable this project, without which none of this would have been possible. In particular a special thank you to

Jack Torrance and Scott Cameron at Baillie Gifford. And at Scottish Widows, Lily Morris, Alison Rinaldi, Lindsay Montgomery, Claire Blyth, April McSkimming and Aaishah Hussain. ◈

Amanda Taylor
Editor, Inspirational Investing
October 2021

Women Are Different

ONE

66

We are committing our money in the hope of earning a financial return, yes. But investing also drives the economy forward... investing is an act of practical hope.

INVESTING: WHEN SHOULD WE START OWNING IT?

Iona Bain

🐦 @IONAYOUNGMONEY
📷 @IONAJBAIN
🔲 YOUNGMONEY
BLOG.CO.UK

IONA BAIN *is an award-winning journalist, broadcaster, speaker and author, and is the UK's go-to voice on millennial money. Since founding the pioneering Young Money Blog in 2011, she's gone on to become one of the most respected financial writers of her generation, with a rare combination of accessibility and authority.*

When is the best time for women to start investing?

This sounds like an essay question, and a trick one at that. When I started writing about money a decade ago, I soon discovered that you can't start laying down the law about what people should do with their money, because everybody's situation is different. And on individual cases, only qualified financial advisers are allowed to formally advise.

So with my excuses now made, let's survey the minefield.

For younger women, our fortunes can too often depend on our access to the Bank of Mum and Dad. As we move into a career, we soon discover a gap widening between those who need maternity and/or caring breaks and those who don't.

For those reaching on tiptoes for the property ladder, investing may look too risky. For the mortgaged it might feel too onerous.

For most there is the big challenge of confidence, not surprising given the barren state of money education in our schools. For the self-employed, the need for a pension looms large.

On top of all that, there's the shadow of Covid-19 and its effect on women.

In March 2021 the Office for National Statistics found women were being furloughed for longer than men and taking on 99% of the childcare.

Then fund group Fidelity reported that 23% of women had lost income over the previous year, 28% were saving less and 17% investing less. It said female-centric industries had borne the brunt of job losses, furlough, and income reductions, while women continued to balance this with more unpaid family care.

Its conclusion was that "encouraging more women to invest just small amounts will be important to ensure that this doesn't result in a permanent step back."

Baroness Helena Morrissey, doyenne of the investment management sector, agrees. Her post-pandemic advice was simple: start investing right now, even if it's only £20 a month.

I know that's a bit like asking any salesman when is the best time to buy – it's always now!

But I think I'll go with Helena, because surely whatever our financial profile, we can afford to lavish £5 a week on our future selves? One thing is certain: the sooner we start, the better.

Why invest rather than just save?

We can't neglect saving, which is right for emergencies and shorter-term goals (attainable within five years) because savings are protected and they can be accessed either instantly or at a predetermined time. Investing comes with no such certainty. Investing is a much riskier, longer ride. But that's why it's perfect for those starting in their 20s and 30s, who have years and decades to wait for their money to grow. Plus, we can take immense satisfaction from the very act of investing.

We are committing our money in the hope of earning a financial return, yes. But investing also drives the economy forward. It helps businesses start up, grow, hire people and provide much-needed services. It helps countries and their citizens become more prosperous. It helps to fund essential infrastructure like roads, bridges, schools and hospitals. It even helps to fund new energy sources to power the world.

As I say in my book *Own It!*, investing is an act of practical hope.

For a start, it helps us fight the demon of inflation. In the wake of the pandemic, big economies including the UK have started to see the return of price inflation on a scale not seen this century. Everything seems to be going up – but at the time of writing savings rates had barely moved from their pathetic sub-1% levels on most accounts.

During the decade from 2010 to 2020, your savings would have been losing money unless they had paid you an average 2.9% a year. That's the rate you would have needed to keep pace with the 37% rise in goods and services. Fast forward to today and it's hotting up – prices rose by 4.7% in the year to August 2021.

Can we really know how stocks will perform?

The past is no guide to the future, as the investment pundits always have to remind us. But it's also the only evidence we have. It suggests that the stock market gives you the best chance of beating inflation – as long as you stay on board for at least five years.

Take the example of someone who was 25 years old in 2005. If they took the plunge and started investing £50 every month in the UK stock market that summer, based on average growth over the 15 year period they would have built up a fund worth almost £12,500 by the summer of 2020, when they hit 40. If they had managed to salt away £100 a month, the pot would have grown to just under £25,000. That's around a third more than the return from an average savings account over the same period.

Investing in shares for any five-year period since 1899 achieved a better return than savings 76% of the time, according to the annual Barclays Equity Gilt Study. Its 2019 report showed that if you extend that to any ten-year period, the chance of outperforming cash savings goes up to an impressive 91%.

When you read about the past performance of an investment, remember it should take inflation into account. For instance, UK shares grew by about 4% a year between 1995 and 2015, after inflation.

A big part of long-term returns comes from the miracle of compounding (earning returns on your returns).

For instance, if you invest £1,000 and receive an annual return of 5%, you'll have £1,050 waiting for you at the end of the first year. But if you leave your money invested, the £1,050 would not grow to £1,100 after year two (as you might think) but to £1,102.50, with the £50 gain from year one generating £2.50 in its own right. This process keeps going.

Assuming constant annual returns of 5%, the same initial investment of £1,000 would grow to almost £1,280 after five years, £1,630 after 10 years and an £3,390 after 25 years.

Of course, your return each year will go up and down, but we have to learn to be okay with the uncertainty of investing. All we can confidently say is that, if the past few decades are anything to go by, taking calculated risks is the best way to grow your money in the long term. *You've got to be in it to win it.* Throughout your investing experience you'll see periodic corrections – these are falls of 10% or more. According to stock market data, they occur around once every 16 months and, on average, last for 43 days. All the more reason that you need to invest for the long term, so you can ride out these bumps and hopefully get back on the upward trail.

Getting *in it to win it*

Two of the issues I explore in *Own It!* are how to launch into investing alongside saving for a home and paying into a pension. The proportion of first-time buyers who had no access to the Bank of Mum and Dad in the 2019–20 financial year was 72%, which was up from 61% three years earlier. For the lucky minority, parents and grandparents gave an average of £19,000 for their deposits in 2020, according to insurer L&G, and only a third were expected to pay any of the cash back.

Helping to level the playing field (a bit) is the Lifetime ISA, where the government pays you £1 for every £4 you save, up to a maximum £4,000 a year (if you're 18 to 39). The cash has to be used to buy a property or you'll pay back the bonus and an extra 5% penalty (at time of writing). But if it is likely to take you five years or more to build that deposit, you could opt for the stocks and shares Lifetime ISA and, if you're able to save more than £333 a month, a regular stocks and shares ISA on top. Hey presto, you're investing.

The pension dilemma is acute for women, whose typical pension pot at age 65 will be a fifth of a man's, according to the Chartered Insurance

Institute. And divorced women typically end up with a pension worth around £26,100, compared to £103,500 for divorced men.

The problem of course is that women miss out on building up their workplace pension because they take more time out of their jobs to look after children or elderly parents, when compared to men. They are also more likely to work part time or rely on their partner's pension, which usually leaves them much worse off should they divorce. In *Own It!* I suggest thinking of it as a *future fund*, whether it be your workplace pension or private/top-up pension or Lifetime ISA. The latter can be used as a pension and thus fills a vital gap for the self-employed.

Stay in, pay more if and when you can, and stay on top of it. I suggest that, if you are also beginning your investing journey, it will help if you get better informed about your pension investing options.

The other big potential dealbreaker for investing newbies is confidence and knowledge – or it used to be. In 2020 share trading became trendy. There was a huge jump in the number of young people buying and selling shares during the Covid-19 lockdown, both in the UK and US. It's all so easy, you just open a free trading account on your phone with a few clicks. You're supposedly on the road to life-changing wins.

And when a few titans like Facebook, Apple, Amazon and Google have accounted for a big proportion of the stock market's gains in recent years, why bother to invest in anything else?

The *Own It!* message is that just because you can trade freely, and everyone on social media is piling in, it doesn't mean you should be beguiled by investing forums like those on Reddit which, by the way, are dominated by men.

These communities stoke the dreaded *fear of missing out.* And these days nothing represents investing FOMO quite like Bitcoin. Its noisy cheerleaders would have you believe the train is leaving the station and you're not on it. But research for the Think Forward Initiative (a Europe-wide financial literacy movement) has shown that the more financially literate you are, the less likely you are to invest in Bitcoin. And guess what, four out of five crypto investors in the UK are male!

But men are surely bossing it in conventional investing – or are they? A study of 2,800 Barclays investors (by Warwick Business School in 2018) found women's portfolios outperforming men's by 1.8% over the previous three years. In investing terms, that's a big gap.

The explanation? Women traded nine times a year on average, compared to 13 times for men – which affects costs – but more importantly they avoided lottery-style investing. Men tended to prefer speculative lower-priced shares which might or might not soar, and they also tended to keep losers and sell winners – counter to classic investing wisdom.

To avoid those pitfalls, you need a cool head – in fact, you need to activate the part of your brain that keeps you cautious, not the bit that makes you reckless, which women are seemingly quite good at.

But in setting your strategy, you also have to avoid being *recklessly cautious*, which means not taking enough risk to produce the returns you could reasonably expect.

Finally, how to do it? Some people have the capacity and curiosity about investing to manage their portfolio in a hands-on way. These investors gravitate towards DIY platforms and trading apps, investing in individual companies and assets. Other people are time-poor and less confident in their ability to beat expert fund managers or the performance of overall stock indices, like the FTSE. They lean on *robo* and real-life advisers, active and passive funds, and/or Exchange Traded Funds. These options aren't automatically more cautious: you can still choose more adventurous versions of them all – I explore it all in *Own It!*

Remember, contrary to what some online investing nerds would have you believe, this isn't a competition. You're not a better, smarter person just because you manage all your own investments. There is nothing wrong with seeking some help, even – or perhaps especially – if you're a more self-assured character who thinks "yeah, I've got this!"

All investors, from beginners upwards, need to be aware of what they don't know. Only then can they work out how to become more enlightened and look for ways to manage their risks.

Ready to take all that on board, girls? Then now is the time to start.

References

Barclays (2019). 'Equity Gilt Study.' Retrieved from ://www.investmentbank.barclays.com/news-and-events/2019-equity-gilt-study.html.

Chartered Insurance Institute (2018). 'Death by a thousand cuts.' Retrieved from www.cii.co.uk/news-items/2018/october/deficit-by-a-thousand-cuts-news.

Legal & General (2020). 'The Bank of Mum and Dad.' Retrieved from www.legalandgeneral.com/landg-assets/adviser/retirement/literature-and-forms/articles-and-reports/BoMaD.pdf.

Montgomery, E.L. (2021). 'The true impact of the pandemic on women's finances.' Retrieved from www.fidelity.co.uk/markets-insights/personal-finance/women-money/the-true-impact-of-the-pandemic-on-womens-finances.

Office for National Statistics (2021). 'An overview of workers who were furloughed in the UK: October 2021.' Retrieved from www.ons.gov.uk/employmentandlabourmarket/peopleinwork/employmentandemployeetypes/articles/anoverviewofworkerswhowerefurloughedintheuk/october2021.

Panos, A.G., Karkkainen, T., & Atkinson, A (2020). 'Financial literacy and attitudes to Cryptocurrencies.' Working papers in Responsible Banking & Finance.

Warwick Business School (2018). 'Are women better investors than men?' Retrieved from www.wbs.ac.uk/news/are-women-better-investors-than-men. ◈

THE BEHAVIOURAL SCIENCE OF INVESTING

What Can We Learn from Gender Differences?

April Vellacott

🐦 @APRIL_VELLACOTT

in LINKEDIN.COM/
IN/VELLACOTT

APRIL VELLACOTT *has been studying the field of human behaviour for a decade, and holds degrees in psychology and behaviour change. She applies this knowledge as a consultant, helping financial services clients to use behavioural science to improve their organisations.*

"

By being aware of how we may make investment decisions differently, we can all begin or, indeed, continue to invest with greater self-knowledge.

April recently co-authored Ripple, The big effects of small behaviour changes in business, *a practical guide for applying behavioural science and nudging in business.*

Gender, investing, and closing the gap: insights from the world of behavioural science

Gender feels like a thorny topic to talk about right now. Especially so if you're making claims about the inherent nature of men, and that of women. Should women win the same prize money as men at Wimbledon, despite not having the same physical endurance? Is it fair to have quotas of women sitting on the boards of large corporations, if there are more talented male candidates? Should female toilets be sacred spaces for cis women, or open to anyone who identifies as female? These are all discussions I've dabbled in over the past few years, and then promptly shied away from at the first sign of tension or disagreement.

But, as thorny as they may be, it's only by talking about these gaps, disparities, and differences that we can begin to overcome them.

About three years into studying behavioural science, I took a module dedicated to gender differences in psychology. Fascinatingly, studies reveal gender differences all over the place, and I found it strangely compulsive to start making sweeping generalisations about men and women. For example, men tend to outperform women when you ask them to mentally rotate objects in their mind, whereas women tend to demonstrate more empathy than men. But, as tempting as it is to divide the world into two neat categories, each with their own superpowers and weaknesses, it's worth saying that when we talk about gender differences in psychology, we're talking about averages over big groups of people.

Some women will have better spatial perception than men, and some men will be more empathetic than women. It's also worth saying that these differences aren't necessarily good or bad. Certain differences may give men the edge in a specific situation, but will hold them back in another. Being aware of the potential differences means we can learn from and compensate for them.

When I first started helping financial services businesses to apply behavioural science to improve their customer experience, it soon became obvious that gender differences extend to financial behaviour. The gender pay gap is now well known, but the pensions gap accumulates over a lifetime of savings opportunities into something far greater. By the time they come to retire, women are likely to have £100,000 less saved in their pension than men.

Compounding this disparity, women are less likely to invest than men: just one in five women currently hold an investment in the UK, compared with one in three men. But, when they do invest, they do better. A study from Warwick Business School looked at male and female investors' returns over three years, and found that women outperformed men by 1.8 percentage points.

Insights from behavioural science could illuminate the source of this difference. There may be persistent features of the way we think that either enhance, or detract from, our investing success. There are some which may hold women back – compared with men, women have fewer role models, tend to avoid losses more, and prefer to take less risk. Equally, there are some which may give women the edge – compared with men, women tend to be less overconfident about their investing abilities, and are less likely to trade their investments too often. Again, to reiterate: these differences are not necessarily good or bad. But being aware of which traits we are more likely to have may increase our self-knowledge, and ultimately help us become better investors.

A lack of role models may deter women from investing

With a lack of visible role models, female investors are more likely to experience imposter syndrome. Imposter syndrome was named to capture how undeserving you feel about your successes, and how hard you might find it to attribute these successes to yourself. Using a measure known as the Imposter Phenomenon Scale, studies have found that women experience more imposter syndrome than men. If women find it much easier to call to mind examples of men who invest and are successful in their field, rather than other women, then we're more likely to experience imposter syndrome. A lack of female role models, therefore, may delay women from making their first steps in investing. And starting to invest late, or failing to invest at all, means that you lose a key ingredient in investing success – time spent in the market.

Women tend to be more loss averse than men

It seems that women are likely to feel losses more intensely than men. If you've ever struggled to give back your Peloton after a 30-day free trial, or suffered through a whole pint of craft beer which you weren't enjoying, you've been trying to avoid a loss. Loss aversion is a well-established concept in behavioural science where we feel losses as more painful than the pleasure from equivalent gains. For example, if you were to lose a £20 note on the street, the pain you would feel would be more acute than the joy you would feel at luckily finding the same note on the same street. Multiple studies have found that women are more loss averse than men, and this can be problematic when it comes to investing.

Rooted in loss aversion, the *disposition effect* is when investors prefer to sell their assets which have gained value, and avoid selling those which have lost value. In other words, you hold underperforming stocks and sell performing ones. Female investors are significantly more likely to behave in this way. As a result, fearing losses may detract from your investing success.

Female investors prefer less risk, hampering long-term gains

Anyone wanting to invest their money has to be willing to take some degree of risk. Some investments are less risky than others, but the highest returns (and, potentially, losses) may go to those who are willing to take the biggest risks. There seem to be gender differences for risk tolerance, ones which may help or hinder female investors.

There are plenty of studies which demonstrate that men and women have significantly different appetites for financial risk and, in general, women prefer less risk than men. And, as Bannier & Neubert have noted, the gender gap in risk preference "is of enormous economic importance." In short, the less risk that women are prepared to take in their investments, the less wealth they can expect in the long run.

Just as this may hamper female investors, it could also be a benefit. Perhaps having a lower tolerance for risk creates female investors who are considered, rather than cautious. If successful investing is partly down to mitigating worst-case scenarios while maximising best-case scenarios, having a lower tolerance for risk is incredibly helpful for the former. And, in the long run, gives returns which are both sustainable and less volatile.

Female investors are less overconfident

Just as there are some features of our psychology which may hold us back, there are others which may boost women's investing tendencies. For example, women may benefit from being less overconfident than men. Overconfidence is where our own confidence in our talent is greater than our actual ability. For example, people tend to think they are better drivers than average, that they can complete tasks in less time than they actually do, and that they are better looking than they really are.

In a study from 2017, Fidelity found that whilst women have less confidence in their investing, their choices outperform those of men. This lack of overconfidence amongst female investors is positive: it might lead to having less concentrated portfolios (which come with higher risks, make us more likely to seek guidance and consider a wide range of perspectives, and motivate us to thoroughly research our investments.

Women benefit from trading less often

When investing, it's easy to mistake activity for achievement: "I'm buying and selling, so I must be adding value." Known as *action bias*, this is our preference to do something, *anything*, rather than do nothing. If you've ever found yourself queuing for coffee in Pret and switching to another, equally slow-moving queue, you've experienced action bias. When it comes to investing behaviour, this bias makes it tempting to trade an investment, rather than hold it.

Women trade less frequently than men, and this could be because women are less likely to experience action bias, something which may occur more with overconfidence. Counterintuitively, doing nothing to your investments is often the best course of action. Trading too often, or abandoning a trading plan, can lead to making rash decisions, incurring extra fees, and wasting time. In short, women may benefit from their predisposition to trade less often.

Knowing your strengths and weaknesses will make you a better investor

Understanding gender differences in decision making can help everyone, male or female, to become a more self-aware investor. Female investors may also be held back by imposter syndrome, making them less likely to invest in the first place. Women seem to feel losses more than men, making them more likely to hold underperforming stocks and sell performing ones. Having a naturally lower inclination for risk may hinder women, with less opportunities for big returns in the long run. Alternatively, a lower risk tolerance might contribute to a more sustainable investing approach.

Proportionately, women's investing styles may benefit in different ways. Women tend to be less overconfident in their investing abilities, leading to a more considered approach, a diversified portfolio, and lower levels of risk and volatility. Linked to this, women trade less frequently than men, saving money and time while avoiding the pitfalls of rushed decisions.

Of course, it would be naïve to make blanket statements about how men always invest in one way, and women in another; investing styles will differ from woman to woman, and from man to man. Some men will be more loss averse than some women, and some women will prefer greater risk than some men. But, by being aware of how we may make investment decisions differently, we can all begin or, indeed, continue to invest with greater self-knowledge.

References

Badawy, R. L., Gazdag, B. A., Bentley, J. R., & Brouer, R. L. (2018). 'Are all impostors created equal? Exploring gender differences in the impostor phenomenon-performance link.' *Personality and Individual Differences*, 131, 156–163.

Bannier, C., & Neubert, M. (2016). 'Gender differences in financial risk taking: The role of financial literacy and risk tolerance.' *Economics Letters*, 145, 130–135.

Barber, B., & Odean, T. (2001). 'Boys will be boys: Gender, overconfidence, and common stock investment.' *The Quarterly Journal of Economics*, 116, 261–292.

Booth, A., & Nolen, P. (2012). 'Gender differences in risk behavior: Does nurture matter?' *The Economic Journal*, 122. F56–F78.

Buehler, R., Griffin, D., & Ross, M. (1994). 'Exploring the "planning fallacy": Why people underestimate their task completion times.' *Journal of Personality and Social Psychology*, 67(3), 366–381.

Charness, G., & Gneezy, U. (2012). 'Strong evidence for gender differences in risk taking.' *Journal of Economic Behavior & Organization*, 83(1), 50–58.

Clance, P. R., & Imes, S. A. (1978). 'The imposter phenomenon in high achieving women: Dynamics and therapeutic intervention.' *Psychotherapy: Theory, Research & Practice*, 15(3), 241–247.

Dohmen, T., Falk, A., Heckman, J., Huffman, D., Schupp, J., Sunde, U., & Wagner, G. (2011). 'Individual risk attitudes: Measurement, determinants, and behavioral consequences.' *Journal of the European Economic Association*, 9, 522–550.

Eisenberg, N. & Lennon, R. (1983). 'Sex differences in empathy and related capacities.' *Psychological Bulletin*, 94, 100–131.

Epley, N., & Whitchurch, E. (2008). 'Mirror, mirror on the wall: Enhancement in self-recognition.' *Personality and Social Psychology Bulletin*, 34(9), 1159–1170.

Gächter, S., Johnson, E., & Herrmann, A. (2007). 'Individual-level loss aversion in riskless and risky choices,' *IZA Working paper*, 35–43.

Kahneman, D., & Tversky, A. (1979). 'Prospect theory: An analysis of decision under risk.' *Econometrica*, 47, 263–291.

Maeda, Y., & Yoon, S. Y. (2013). 'A meta-analysis on gender differences in mental rotation ability measured by the purdue spatial visualization tests: visualization of rotations (psvt:r).' *Educational Psychology Review*, 25, 69–94.

Odean, T. (1998). 'Volume, volatility, price, and profit when all traders are above average.' *Journal of Finance*, 53(6), 1887–1934.

Pallier, G., Wilkinson, R., Danthiir, V., Kleitman, S., Knezevic, G., Stankov, L., & Roberts, R. D. (2002). 'The role of individual differences in the accuracy of confidence judgments.' *Journal of General Psychology*, 129(3), 257–299.

Rau, H.A., (2014). 'The disposition effect and loss aversion: Do gender differences matter?' *Economics Letters*, 123(1), 33–36.

Rieger, M., Wang, M., & Hens, T. (2011). 'Prospect theory around the world.' *NHH Dept. of Finance & Management Science Discussion Paper.*

Scottish Widows (2020). 'Let's call time on the #Genderpensiongap.' Retrieved from www.scottishwidows.co.uk/yourfuture.

Shefrin, H., & Statman, M. (1985). 'The disposition to sell winners too early and ride losers too long: Theory and evidence.' *The Journal of Finance,* 40, 777–790.

Svenson, O. (1981). 'Are we all less risky and more skillful than our fellow drivers?' *Acta Psychologica,* 47(2), 143–148.

Warwick Business School (2018). 'Are women better investors than men?' Retrieved from www.wbs.ac.uk/news/are-women-better-investors-than-men.

Zeelenberg, M., Van den Bos, K., Van Dijk, E., & Pieters, R. (2002). 'The inaction effect in the psychology of regret.' *Journal of Personality and Social Psychology,* 82(3), 314–327.

GENDER AND FINANCIAL RISK TAKING

Dr Ylva Baeckström

☒ YLVABAECKSTROM.COM

DR YLVA BAECKSTRÖM

is a researcher in finance at King's College London and an experienced banker, entrepreneur, psychotherapist, author and public speaker. Ylva's research interests are in gender and intersectionality in finance, aiming to contribute to positive change that fosters equality in financial services and beyond.

" Women are not born with 'low investment risk tolerance' – it was created by society. Risk needs to be reframed and investment options properly explained to give women an equal opportunity to generate future wealth.

Prior to academia, Ylva was the CEO of a fintech start up and a senior banker. Her research is published in highly ranked academic journals like the Journal of Corporate Finance *and* Journal of Economic Behavior and Organization. *Her book* Gender and Finance: Addressing Inequality in Financial Services *is published by Routledge in 2022. She gave a TEDx talk `Run like the real woman you are' in 2020. Ylva is passionate about delivering impactful research that drives change at an individual, organisational and policy level to improve financial equality to benefit the whole of society.*

Gender inequality in lifetime earnings

We are all too aware of the headline problems that women face with relation to their lifetime incomes. Women typically earn less than men during their careers. This inequality widens as education and seniority levels rise, meaning that women with high educational levels, and those who reach senior management positions, are penalised financially for doing so. Women are much more likely than men to take on caregiving roles: as parents or caring for relatives. These unpaid roles include women picking up the physical and mental load of household management, thus supporting their husbands to enable them to focus on their careers. They often involve taking multi-year career breaks, and transitioning to part-time roles to balance these additional commitments. Women therefore accumulate far less employment income compared to men during their working lives.

When the total income of men and women is taken into account these differences become even wider. This is because women typically have fewer investments and traditionally inherit less, meaning men enjoy much higher income from capital such as property and other investments (The World Economic Forum, 2020).

This gender inequality in *employment* and *total* income unsurprisingly means women have less money available to invest or save towards their retirement. Men accumulate more wealth than women, and subsequently this gender-based income inequality extends to, and then worsens during retirement. Evidence shows that the majority of the UK public currently do not save enough to fund their retirement (FCA, 2017) with 55% of working age adults feeling that they do not understand enough about pensions to make investment decisions (Money and Pensions Service, 2019). In my research I find that only a very small minority of people have any idea about how large their retirement pots need to be in order to fund their desired lifestyle (Baeckström, 2020). A particularly vulnerable group is women, who on average live longer than men (83 versus 79 years; WHO, 2016). Women are less likely to hold a pension (Cumbo, 2017) and, when they do, tend to make a lower allocation to risky assets (Agnew et al., 2008; Rabener, 2017) which have lower return potential compared to higher risk investments. Consequently, women's pensions tend to be both smaller and produce lower returns compared to men's.

The cumulative effects of the gender income gap, combined with gender differences in investment behaviour, result in women retiring with up to 40% lower pension income relative to men (UK statistics: Hawthorne, 2018).

Disappointingly, policy making remains stubbornly gender unequal. For example, the automatic enrolment introduced in the UK in 2012 means that 73% of employed people have the right to receive pension contributions from their employers (increased from 47% in 2012: ONS, 2018). However, the savings rate of 8% is equal for both genders.

Because a woman earns less, if she invests an equal percentage of her earnings, she ends up investing a much smaller amount. If she also invests in lower-risk assets, the cumulative effect on her retirement is dismal. Auto enrolment further excludes the self employed and those who earn less than £10,000 (GOV.UK, 2020), the majority of whom are women.

Gender and risk taking

Women are generally assumed to have preferences that lead them to exhibit more conservative behaviour compared to men. Indeed, research evidences how men tend to take higher risks than women in a wide range of activities. This is particularly prevalent in traditionally masculine domains (Byrnes, Miller, & Schafer, 1999; Beyer & Bowden, 1997), many of which require a quantitative skill set. This is frequently cited as a partial explanation for the persistent under-representation of women in certain professions, for example engineering and information technology.

Gender and investment decision making

Financial investing requires quantitative skills.

When it comes to dealing with financial matters and investing there are on average real differences in the attitudes and behaviour of men and women. But the current standard theories of financial behaviour do not take this into account. Neither traditional economic theory nor modern portfolio theory mention gender as an important variable to determine a suitable asset allocation strategy. These theories assume that people make rational investment choices which maximise the return on their investment based on their risk preferences (Markowitz, 1952).

However, individual investors tend to rely on their own perceptions and intuitive beliefs when making investment decisions, rather than selecting efficient portfolios that optimally balance risk and reward (Benartzi & Thaler, 2001; Kahneman, 2003). Investment decisions are therefore strongly influenced by emotions, rather than rational thinking. This renders people (regardless of gender) prone to biased decision making. However, women are more likely to feel *fear* while men feel *anger* when faced with risky investment choices. Fear can make women shy away from taking risks while anger can unlock more risky behaviour (Loewenstein, Weber, Hsee & Welch, 2001) and an action-based approach.

There is ample evidence that men take more investment risks than women, a difference that disadvantages women. The academic literature documents lower investment risk tolerance (Baeckström, Marsh & Silvester, 2021; Charness & Gneezy, 2012), lower levels of financial literacy (Bucher-Koenen et al., 2017; Dwyer, Gilkeson, & List, 2002; Lusardi & Mitchell, 2007), and less confidence (Barber & Odean, 2001; Croson & Gneezy, 2009; Estes & Hosseini, 1988) among female investors. These gender differences extend to investment behaviour, whereby women make more conservative asset allocation decisions and hold more cash in their retirement portfolios (Charness & Gneezy, 2012; Eckel & Füllbrunn, 2015; Sunden & Surette, 1998).

It is therefore widely believed that women both judge themselves to be more risk averse and make more conservative investment choices than men (Eckel & Grossman, 2008). This can act as a self-fulfilling prophecy whereby women invest less, and because they have lower risk tolerance they make more conservative investment decisions than men. Lower levels of knowledge and confidence about making investment decisions can provide some explanation as to why women keep more of their savings in cash and feel less able or motivated to focus on securing their financial futures.

These gender differences are seen in the judgements that women make about themselves and also in the judgements that finance professionals make about their female clients, when they encourage women to invest less than they need (Baeckström, Marsh & Silvester, 2021).

One immediate problem with the financial services industry pandering to these perceived preferences, is that women end up holding more cash in their investment portfolios rather than higher risk, higher return assets. This is particularly damaging in a low interest rate/high inflation environment where cash savings do not have any real earnings potential. Not investing sufficiently and not being advised to invest sufficiently means women are losing money.

Exceptions

However, these differences are not applicable to all women or men in our society and there is a dearth of research about people who identify with other diverse genders. There are many exceptions to the gender-based assumptions that we make about ourselves and others. Wealth, profession and financial advice can be important contributing factors. Research demonstrates that women who are senior managers or entrepreneurs may exhibit higher risk-taking attributes (Fisher & Yao, 2017) and that wealthy women feel they have the same knowledge and confidence in their investment abilities as men (Baeckström, Marsh & Silvester, 2021). Literature also shows how having a female, instead of a male, financial adviser can make a difference for women. Women with female financial advisors are found to invest much (11%!) more and feel more confident and knowledgeable about their investment decisions (Baeckström, Marsh and Silvester, 2021). However, there is a scarcity of client facing finance professionals who are women; only about 15% of financial advisers and 10% of fund managers are female (Bellstrom and Hinchliffe, 2019).

Research therefore challenges the blanket assumption that *all* women are more conservative than men. Risk tolerance needs to be considered a situational trait that does not apply to all women, or at all times. Other personal characteristics, a woman's situation and indeed how women are treated (by the financial services industry) might matter even more than gender when it comes to investment attitudes and behaviour.

Women are not born with 'low investment risk tolerance' – it was created by society. Risk needs to be reframed and investment options properly explained to give women an equal opportunity to generate future wealth.

Positives and negatives

More conservative attitudes and behaviours in relation to investment decisions have disadvantages and advantages. They can be disadvantageous for women's wealth accumulation when women do not invest enough or miss higher returns by not taking sufficient investment risk. However, in situations when women invest actively, the returns on their investment portfolios are often higher than those of men, simply because men are more prone to overconfidence bias.

Overconfidence is actually more damaging to portfolio performance than conservatism. Researchers who analysed the buy and sell patterns of over 35,000 individual investors over a 6-year period found that overconfident behaviour among men saw them trading 1.5 times more, and holding portfolios that produced 1% lower returns than women's portfolios (Barber & Odean, 2001). Overconfident men tend to buy and sell too many assets in their portfolios, too often. They therefore pay much higher transaction costs, which eat into their investment return.

There is further evidence that professional female fund managers outperform their male counterparts (Bliss & Potter, 2002) despite adopting less risk in the funds they manage (Niessen-Ruenzi & Ruenzi, 2017). Equally, researchers show how having at least three women on corporate boards is associated with better performance over a number of measures in Fortune 500 companies. And having more women in senior leadership teams is associated with higher revenues, increased return on assets and reduced staff turnover. In contrast, non-diverse, male only leadership teams and boards can induce homogeneous decision making, overconfident risk taking and potentially disastrous concentrated positions – similar to the overconfident stock trading behaviour identified by Barber and Odean.

So, women who do invest definitively have the abilities to build and manage portfolios that produce good returns both for themselves and when managing money for their clients. And women who enter senior leadership and director positions contribute to better performing organisations – financially and for their employees and customers.

Why are men and women different when it comes to taking investment risk?

Women are not genetically predisposed to be less knowledgeable, less confident, or less risk tolerant when investing their own money or when they apply their skills in business and entrepreneurial ventures. Instead, society created these negative gender traits during the socialisation process. This gender socialisation process starts at birth and follows the girl and woman throughout her life. We, all of us in society, push our preconceived ideas of what is female and what is male onto children and adults. This results in gender stereotype formation and stereotype treatment.

But stereotypes are not based on facts. For example, it is society that created the expectation that boys underperform girls in maths. Perhaps because we underestimate girls and disregard their documented maths outperformance during primary school (Adams, 2019), girls are found to lose confidence in their maths abilities by the time they reach secondary school, when they begin to score lower than boys in exams (Perez-Felkner, Nix & Thomas, 2017). This lack of confidence in their quantitative abilities can lead to girls and women avoiding quantitative domains, including personal investing or pursuing careers in financial services. Women are therefore at risk of living up to the negative gender stereotype expectations that others hold about them, expectations that do not correspond to the wiring of their brains. This is because in contrast to one's biological sex, gender is not biological: gender differences are largely created through our social interactions.

I suggest that women feel less skilled and confident in traditionally male domains, like investing, because others expect them to be. They were socialised that way. These problems are entrenched in culture and maintained through government and corporate policy making. Unfortunately the negative gender stereotype expectations held by others can become internalised by women, who limit their own performance potential as a result.

Unfair, unsustainable and unsurprising

When it comes to money and investing, women haven't been well served by government policies. While women in the developed world now have *most* of the legal rights they need to participate in the economic system, the vast majority of countries still have at least one national level policy that excludes women from full participation. In many developed world economies, e.g., the US and the UK, women did not gain the legal rights to fully participate in the economic system until the 1970s or the 1980s. Women in the UK were unable to open bank accounts in their own name until 1973. Nor could they become members of stock exchanges until 1967 in the US (New York Stock Exchange) or 1973 in the UK (London Stock Exchange) or apply for credit until 1980 in the UK.

Women continue to be disadvantaged in terms of access to credit and bank accounts. In 72 out of 153 countries surveyed by the World Economic Forum, certain groups of women still lacked the legal rights to open a bank account or obtain credit in 2020. And in 25 countries women's inheritance rights were inferior to those of men.

Clearly the Covid-19 pandemic removed much of the progress made over the last few years, with gender inequality taking giant backwards strides in all areas of life, everywhere. Global events such as the Covid-19 pandemic have the potential to hinder the progress made in gender equality across many areas of life.

Explicit Implicit Associations

Over half a million people from 34 countries have completed the Implicit Association Test, which measures our gender based attitudes (bias) in a range of domains. Over 70% of us associate concepts like science or maths more with men than women. These deeply embedded stereotypes mean that we *expect* men to be naturally more gifted and perform better in the real world domains that feel quantitative. My research shows how people, regardless of their own gender association or background, tend to associate finance, investing, leadership, entrepreneurship and risk taking significantly more with the male than the female gender. This means that when faced with a woman in those domains we tend to be more surprised about seeing her there, and on some level she may feel the same (Baeckström, 2020).

We associate money and investing with the male gender.

So, the world of financial services was created by men, for men. Its culture is stereotypically alpha male, its language and jargon unappealing to most people regardless of their gender association: female, male or another diverse gender. This has resulted in men, particularly alpha males, being predisposed to be more confident about their investment abilities, and to feel that the financial world and investing are naturally for them. In contrast many women feel that they do not belong in the financial world. Exclusion combined with stereotype expectations instead make it understandable that many women lack confidence, and feel that they know less about financial investing, which in turn makes it difficult to find motivation to focus on their personal finances. This is compounded by women and others around them *assuming* they have lower levels of financial literacy compared to men. Inevitably, women therefore have less confidence in their ability to make investment decisions.

What can women do to challenge this?

1. **Avoid living up to the negative gender stereotypes held by others around you.** Gender differences in investment behaviour are driven by outdated and limiting attitudes and behaviour. Not all men and women are the same. There are exceptions and gender attitudes are elastic and can change. Do not allow outdated expectations to limit your performance and abilities.

2. **The real risk is not investing.** Taking responsibility to ensure that we have enough money to fund our retirement is crucial. Women have to pay extra attention to this because they earn less than men during their lifetime and therefore have less money to invest. As women live longer than men they need more, not less, money at retirement. The government and the financial services industry are not going to do this for you. Everyone needs to take responsibility for their own finances.

3. **Reduce the gap.** Women who focus on securing their financial futures will challenge negative gender stereotypes, increase their lifetime savings and secure their retirement incomes. Every woman who does this will contribute to reducing the societal financial gender inequality gap.

4. **Confidence ≠ Competence.** Just because a woman lacks in confidence when it comes to investing, that doesn't mean she lacks in competence. Equally, male overconfidence is not a winner; the right level of confidence is the one that unlocks the motivation to focus on your personal finances.

5. **Learn and take action.** For many regardless of their gender, investing is perceived as complex and therefore difficult to understand. Learn more – increased knowledge enables positive action. Reduce your financial anxiety by taking action.

6. **Ask for help.** A financial adviser could help navigate the complex pensions landscape and access tax-efficient savings. Financial advice can assist people in making better investment decisions that increase how much they have to live on in retirement. If you prefer to work with a female financial adviser, demand one.

References

Adams, R. (2019) 'Gap in academic skills of girls and boys widens, show SATs.' Retrieved from www.theguardian.com/education/2019/sep/05/gap-in-academic-skills-of-girls-and-boys-widens-show-sats.

Agnew, J.R., Anderson, L.R., Gerlach, J.R., & Szykman, L.R. (2008). 'Who Chooses Annuities? An Experimental Investigation of the Role of Gender, Framing, and Defaults.' *American Economic Review*, 98, 418–422.

Baeckström, Y. (2020). 'Investing to secure your financial future - 4 November 2019.' Retrieved from www.kcl.ac.uk/events/investing-to-secure-your-financial-future.

Baeckström, Y., Marsh, I. & Silvester, J. (2021). 'Variations in Investment Advice Provision: A Study of Financial Advisers of Millionaire Investors.' *Journal of Economic Behavior & Organization*, 188, 716–735.

Baeckström, Y., Marsh, I. & Silvester, J. (2021). 'Financial advice and gender: wealthy individual investors in the UK.' *Journal of Corporate Finance*, 71.

Barber, B.M., & Odean, T. (2001). 'Boys Will Be Boys: Gender, Overconfidence, and Common Stock Investment.' *Quarterly Journal of Economics*, 116, 261-292.

Bellstrom, K., & Hinchliffe, E. (2019). 'Why More Clients Want Female Financial Advisers: The Broadsheet.' Retrieved from fortune.com/2019/08/27/female-financial-advisers.

Benartzi, S., & Thaler, R.H. (2001). 'Naïve Diversification Strategies in Defined Contribution Saving Plans.' *American Economic Review*, 91(1), 79–98.

Beyer, S., & Bowden, E. M. (1997). 'Gender Differences in Self-Perceptions: Convergent Evidence from Three Measures of Accuracy and Bias.' *Personality and Social Psychology Bulletin*, 23(2), 157–172.

Bliss, R.T., & Potter, M.E. (2002). 'Mutual fund managers: Does gender matter?' *Journal of Business and Economic Studies*, 8(1), 1–15.

Bucher-Koenen et al., (2017). 'How Financially Literate Are Women? An Overview and New Insights.' *NBER Working Paper Series.*

Byrnes, J. P., Miller, D. C., & Schafer, W. D. (1999). 'Gender differences in risk taking: a meta-analysis.' *Psychological Bulletin*, 125, 367–383.

Charness, G., & Gneezy, U. (2012) 'Strong Evidence for Gender Differences in Risk Taking.' *Journal of Economic Behavior & Organisation*, 83(1), 50–58.

Croson, R., & Gneezy, U. (2009) 'Gender Differences in Preferences.' *Journal of Economic Literature*, 47(2), 448–474.

Cumbo, J. (2017). Retrieved from www.ft.com/content/c9b74996-b582-11e7-aa26-bb002965bce8.

Dwyer, P.D., Gilkeson, J.H., & List, J.A., (2002) 'Gender differences in revealed risk taking: evidence from mutual fund investors.' *Economics Letters*, 76(2), 151–158.

Eckel, C.C., & Füllbrunn, S.C. (2015) 'Thar SHE Blows? Gender, Competition, and Bubbles in Experimental Asset Markets.' *American Economic Review*, 105(2), 906–920.

Eckel, C., & Grossman, P., (2008); 'Differences in the Economic Decisions of Men and Women: Experimental Evidence.' *Handbook of Experimental Economics Results*, Chapter 57, 1(4), 509–519.

Estes, R., & Hosseini, J. (1988). 'The Gender Gap on Wall Street: An Empircal Analysis of Confidence in Investment Decision Making.' *The Journal of Psychology: Interdisciplinary and Applied*, 122(6), 577–590.

Financial Conduct Authority (2017). 'Understanding the financial lives of UK adults: Findings from the FCA's Financial Lives Survey 2017.' Retrieved from www.fca.org.uk/publication/research/financial-lives-survey-2017.pdf.

Fisher, P.J, & Yao, R. (2017). 'Gender Differences in Financial Risk Tolerance.' *Journal of Economic Psychology*, 61, 191–202.

Gallup (2014). 'The Business Benefits of Gender Diversity.' Retrieved from www.gallup.com/workplace/236543/business-benefits-gender-diversity.aspx.

GOV.UK. 'Workplace pensions.' Retrieved from www.gov.uk/workplace-pensions.

Gustafson, P. (1998). 'Gender differences in risk perception: Theoretical and methodological perspectives.' *Risk Analysis*, 18(6), 805–811.

Hawthorne, S. (2018). 'Pensions Gender Pay Gap reaches 40 per cent.' Retrieved from www.pensions-expert.com/DB-Derisking/Pensions-gender-pay-gap-reaches-40-per-cent.

Herman, L. (2021). 'The Cold, Hard Proof That More Women Means Better Business.' Retrieved from www.themuse.com/advice/the-cold-hard-proof-that-more-women-means-better-business.

Kahneman, D. (2003). 'A Perspective on Judgment and Choice: Mapping Bounded Rationality. *American Psychologist*, 58(9), 697–720.

Loewenstein, G. F., Weber, E. U., Hsee, C. K., & Welch, N. (2001). 'Risk as Feelings.' *Psychological Bulletin*, 127, 267–286.

Lusardi, A., & Mitchell, O., (2007) 'Financial Literacy and Retirement Preparedness: Evidence and Implications for Financial Education.' *Business Economics*, 42(1), 35–44.

Markowitz, H. (1952). 'Portfolio Selection.' *Journal of Finance*, 7(1), 77–91.

McKinsey & Company (2015). 'Why diversity matters.' Retrieved from www.mckinsey.com/business-functions/organization/our-insights/why-diversity-matters.

Money and Pensions Service (2019). 'Listening Document.' Retrieved from moneyandpensionsservice.org.uk/wp-content/uploads/2019/04/Listening-Document.pdf.

Niessen-Ruenzi, A., & Ruenzi, S. (2017). 'Sex Matters: Gender Bias in the Mutual Fund Industry.' Retrieved from papers.ssrn.com/sol3/papers.cfm?abstract_id=1957317.

Perez-Felkner, L., Nix, S. & Thomas, K. (2017). Retrieved from blog.frontiersin.org/2017/04/24/under-challenge-girls-confidence-level-not-math-ability-hinders-path-to-science-degrees.

Project Implicit, 'Implicit Association Test.' Retrieved from: implicit.harvard.edu/implicit/takeatest.html.

ONS (2018). 'Pension participation at record high but contributions cluster at minimum levels.' Retrieved from www.ons.gov.uk/employmentandlabourmarket/peopleinwork/workplacepensions/articles/pensionparticipationatrecordhighbutcontributionsclusterat minimumlevels/2018-05-04.

Rabener, E. (2017). 'Investors Still Don't Understand Investment Risk.' Retrieved from uk.scalable.capital/assets/3x3i7a9xgm11/6iXUqtjAkMg2MSGGaSCGKq/f35a35ac3522a053cdb0cf06a3b1188f/Research_Investors_Still_Dont_Understand_Investment_Risk.pdf

Sunden, A.E., & Surette, B.J. (1998). 'Gender Differences in the Allocation of Assets in Retirement Savings Plans.' *American Economic Review*, 88(2), 207–211.

World Economic Forum (2020). 'COVID-19 has widened the gender poverty gap, says the UN.' Retrieved from www.weforum.org/agenda/2020/09/covid19-women-pandemic-gender-poverty-gap-united-nations.

World Health Organization (2016). 'Life expectancy and healthy life expectancy data by country.' Retrieved from apps.who.int/gho/data/node.main.688 ◈

Investment Planning

TWO

"

Anyone who gives you a specific tip about one thing to back or buy should be ignored – boring diversified investments are what most of us need!

FINANCIAL ADVICE

What Are the Options and What Does It Cost?

Holly Mackay

🐦 📷 @HOLLYAMACKAY

◪ BORING
MONEY.CO.UK

HOLLY MACKAY *has worked in finance since 1999. She is a financial expert, a commentator on investment markets and the founder and MD of Boring Money. She likes translating financial gobbledygook into real speak and trying to help people without PhDs in finance to make sensible decisions with minimum pain.*

Holly read Modern Languages at Oxford, specialising in Medieval French, which obviously made her immediately highly employable. She went backpacking in Australia, worked in TV for a while and then decided that TV was boring but the stock market was awesomely interesting. She held senior roles at Merrill Lynch, Aviva and Santander before setting up her first business, The Platforum, in 2008.

She sold the business to Centaur Media and left in 2014, launching Boring Money in July 2015.

Holly is a regular media commentator and has appeared on or contributed to the BBC, the Times, *the* Telegraph *and the* Mail on Sunday. *She is living proof that you can be in Set 4 for maths when you're 13 and still get your head around investments.*

Traditional advice – what does it cost?

Taking on financial advice through the traditional channels can look a bit intimidating. Only one in ten people say they use a financial adviser currently. Of those who don't, half say they would consider using one in the future. Potential investors are put off by barriers such as: not knowing if advice is right for them, uncertainty about what advisers actually do, and the difficulty of finding a reliable adviser. However, the world of financial advice has become much more transparent and inclusive in recent years, so there has never been a better time to explore it.

Let's start with costs.

First things first, any initial meeting which is an introduction should be free – you are both deciding if you can work together. In this first session you'll generally be asked to give an indicator of how much money you have available to invest. To be blunt, if you have less than £75,000 in savings and pensions, advisers are going to find it hard to charge a fee which makes it worth their time but isn't eating up a crazily large amount of your savings.

Expect to pay an upfront fee for advice and the implementation of the strategy you will agree with your adviser, with further costs on an ongoing basis. This initial fee can often be up to 3% of the sum invested. Once you are up and running most advisers will charge you between 1% and 2% a year for the full ongoing service – this includes their advice, all administration, and all investments and pension products.

Fees are falling as some providers get smarter at using technology to do much of the heavy lifting – new hybrid advice firm Netwealth for example, offers blended services which are part-digital and part-personal – and they charge a lower ongoing fee, shaking up the pack.

Increasingly, more people say they would prefer to pay a fixed fee for receiving financial advice – 38% would prefer a fixed fee, compared to just 13% who would prefer to pay a percentage fee (and 49% said they don't know, showing just how confusing people find this).

Fixed fees are generally charged based on the complexity of your affairs. Often in the fixed-fee world, once you're set up and would like more regular communication, your adviser will price up a package, which may include a review meeting, ongoing monitoring of your plans, and access to further advice. You can also search for one-off services which tackle specific needs – inheritance tax, retirement planning, general MOTs, etc. These one-off packages vary but could cost between about £1,000 and £2,000.

Some firms will undertake a project for an hourly fee, roughly priced at £150 to £300 per hour.

What are some alternative options?

If traditional services don't appeal, you have more options than ever when it comes to getting some advice.

It's worth mentioning the government-funded PensionWise – only for those aged 50+, it offers a call with someone who can take all of your pensions questions and give you some help. The call takes about 45 minutes and is completely free. They can't give you personalised advice (e.g., what stocks to buy, what products to open, or where to move your money) but they will talk you through your choices, and it's a very good start. We all like a freebie – and this is a reputable freebie!

Financial coaching

For those still some way off retirement and trying to get their heads around their long-term savings, financial coaching is an interesting option to consider. For an annual fee of about £150–£200, which is normally charged monthly (packages vary depending on what services you want) you can engage a financial coach to help you work through your finances.

These coaches are not regulated to give financial advice, so they can't just give you a plan and tell you what to do. But they will point out what you need to consider, where any tax breaks are, how to structure and set up a pension, how to start investing, and more generally, point out if you are being a wally! It's also worth trying to persuade your employer to support this – if you can pay through salary sacrifice it becomes cheaper. Check out Claro or Octopus Moneycoach.

Digital advice

If you can't quite face the prospect of learning about your money options and want someone to take that pain away, but you cannot afford the gold-plated solutions, then check out digital advice. There are some evolving services that get computers to do a lot of the heavy lifting, and some that reinforce this with genuine human beings who will take your questions along the way.

The idea is that a decent investment portfolio is something that a computer can set up and maintain – and this could actually be *more* robust than a person making individual decisions without the same degree of governance and controls. At the same time, we all like speaking to a person for that final reassurance we're not doing anything drastic with hidden consequences.

Another aspect of digital advice is convenience – you can sit at your computer with a glass of wine in hand, in a tracksuit with unwashed hair. And a computer cannot judge you or patronise you!

Expect to pay less than 1% a year all-in – that includes advice, admin and all investments. Expecting a cost of about £80–£100 a year for every £10,000 you have is a good yardstick.

Our digital advice tables on boringmoney.co.uk/advice can help you pick a provider that is right for you. They range from those focused on helping typically younger people with smaller balances and simpler needs (have a look at OpenMoney) to those aimed at helping older folk navigate their way along the murky path to retirement (check out abrdn, Hub or Vanguard). More banks are moving into this space – Barclays has led the pack here, offering these services to its current account customers.

What to ask an adviser and what to look for

1. How much? Give them the total of your savings and ask them to give you an indicator of set-up and ongoing costs – in £s if you prefer.

2. What do they specialise in. Not all advisers will do final salary scheme pension transfers, for example.

3. Qualifications are one way to review and sort. Generally, the three letters CFP denoting a Certified Financial Planner or (rather confusingly) Chartered Financial Planner are well worth looking out for. They don't necessarily indicate a brilliant adviser who will be right for you – but they do indicate someone who has done some hard exams, put in the legwork, and swotted up on all the technical stuff.

4. Are they bona fide? Do check that your financial adviser is registered with the regulator – the FCA. They have an online register of regulated financial advisers and it doesn't take long to check.

5. For those of you who are very focused on sustainability, we hear more about how our pensions and investments can be agents of change. It's a new area in finance, but some advisers have the ESG certificate from the CFA and, trust me, they will know more about Environmental, Social, and Governance-focused investing than you will ever want to!

6. Gender? We also know that more and more women want to speak to a female financial adviser. If you're going to go through the financial intricacies of divorce, for example, it's very hard to do without pulling out the Kleenex. It's less embarrassing to do that in front of a woman (in my experience!) and there are more women who actually specialise in this specific area, for example. So do search for female advisers if this matters to you.

7. Word of mouth. It's such a personal relationship that recommendations are important. Look at what existing clients have said, and try to read content or articles from your adviser. Are they on Twitter or social media? Do they sound like someone you would trust with your family's money? Money's personal – I think it's important to get an adviser you actually like!

On a final note, at Boring Money we have built a whole new section on our website which covers all your advice options, showcases providers and individual advisers, and should help you to unearth some great solutions to give you the advice you can afford and need.

The good news is that we all have more choice and more transparency than ever. The bad news is that social media has given more airtime to more people who use their mouths more than their ears. Do take any so-called financial influencer with a very large pinch of salt. Anyone can share a story about one thing they backed which did really well. They don't tell you about all the things they backed which flopped. In my experience anyone who gives you a specific tip about one thing to back or buy should be ignored – boring, diversified investments are what most of us need! Good luck.

References

Boring Money Advice Report. Retrieved from www.boring moneybusiness.co.uk/reports/advice-report-2021. ◈

"

One of my favourite parts
of my job is sitting down
with clients and working
out what is important to
them in life.

HOW TO SPOT A GOOD FINANCIAL ADVISER

An Adviser's Point of View

Lisa Conway-Hughes

@MISSLOLLYMONEY

@LOLLY_LISA

LADIESFINANCE
CLUB.COM

LISA CONWAY-HUGHES *is a chartered financial planner and a fellow of the Personal Finance Society. Lisa joined the financial industry 16 years ago and in October 2020 was voted Financial Adviser of the Year and Marketing Influencer of the Year – London by Professional Adviser Magazine WIFA.*

Lisa, also known as Miss Lolly, writes, speaks, tweets, and blogs on all things money related. Lisa is passionate about making financial education open to all and loves taking the jargon out of the financial world. Lisa is the author of Money Lessons and features regularly as a media expert in the female press and newspapers as well as having been interviewed by the BBC News. Lisa has been featured in Red, Good Housekeeping, Stylist, *the* Financial Times, *the* Times, *the* Telegraph *and many more.*

Lisa also co-hosts the Ladies Finance Club podcast with Molly Benjamin and together they run the Ladies Finance Club UK.

There are lots of times in our lives where getting advice from a professional can make a big difference. You might be asking yourself in what situations should you seek financial advice and who should that advice come from. Then once you've decided to get some support, how on earth do you go about finding the right adviser? As an adviser myself, I'll try to answer some of these questions.

Why get advice?

So in what situations might you need financial advice? Following are some examples of lifestyle changes and milestones where a financial adviser could help you:

- Opening a pension or consolidating multiple pensions.
- Investing.
- Buying property.
- Setting up and running a business.
- Retirement planning.
- Marriage.
- Divorce.

- Starting a family.

- Changing career.

- Any situation where you need to take out a financial product (mortgage, insurance, pension etc.,).

If you find yourself in any of these situations, a financial adviser can help you make informed decisions with your money. Once you've decided to engage an adviser, you will need to choose one to work with, so let's look at how you can make that choice.

Choosing an adviser

When choosing an adviser I think it is really important to do your own research before you dive in! Most of my new clients come through recommendations from existing clients or their accountants. This is always a great compliment to me, but I think the individual should be careful and not rely solely on these recommendations.

There are lots of contributing factors that will make a financial adviser the one for you. Here are my top four:

1. Qualifications

2. Experience

3. Personality

4. Independence

Qualifications

Qualifications are obviously very important, and you could say that as a Chartered Adviser and a Fellow of the Personal Finance Society I am biased. But for me, it was important to invest time in myself to demonstrate my knowledge and also to learn more. To maintain my qualifications, I have to demonstrate high levels of continued professional development each year, ensuring my knowledge remains up to date and relevant. This gives me the confidence I need to know my clients are in good hands.

Experience

So why might you not choose a well-qualified adviser? The answer to this is that experience speaks volumes. It's important to understand how long someone has been advising and who they usually advise. I know my strengths lie in helping clients in the accumulation phase of their lives and I love doing what I am good at.

Personality

Personality plays a big part, I believe, in how well I am able to best help clients. If I am not speaking their language, it is going to be difficult to get under the client's skin and *really* understand them. One of my favourite parts of my job is sitting down with clients and working out what is important to them in life. If I don't feel comfortable enough to ask (often quite personal) questions, I am not going to be able to understand a client as well as I would like, which makes it difficult for me to advise on the best solutions for the client.

Independence

Finally it is important that you understand an adviser's motivation to help you. Whose side are they on? In my early career I worked as a tied adviser and although I felt I did a good job for clients, it still niggled me that perhaps I could do a better job if I was independent. Being independent means that you can advise a client on any regulated products that are out there in the market, whereas *tied* means you have a set menu of providers whose products you can sell. The last part of that sentence is the most important for me. Am I an adviser or am I selling? Hence, it was important to me to become independent. ◈

MAKING YOUR PLAN: AN INVESTING CHECKLIST

Becky O'Connor

🐦 @REBECCAOCO

◩ GOOD-WITH-MONEY.COM

BECKY O'CONNOR *is Head of Pensions and Savings for interactive investor. Becky co-founded Good With Money, an ethical and sustainable personal finance website, in 2015. A former financial journalist, Becky is also chair of the Castlefield independent ethical advisory committee, and a fellow of the Royal Society of Arts.*

"

What is your goal for your investment? How much does it cost? When do you need that money by? Getting clear on your goals and timelines will help you make the best decisions for your future.

Investing checklist

Investing effectively can be a complex undertaking, but everyone needs to start somewhere. Here are some of the key considerations you will need to bear in mind when you take that first step on your investing journey:

1. Work out what you are investing for

What is your goal for your investment? How much does it cost? When do you need that money by? Getting clear on your goals and timelines will help you make the best decisions for your future. If it is something more than three years away, investing could be a good strategy. Any amount needed sooner than three years counts as a savings rather than an investment goal. Ideally, you'd be looking at investing over a time frame of five to ten years, so it might be a longer-term thing than you are used to. Divide the amount you need by the number of months you will be investing for to give a rough monthly amount to invest initially. With investment growth, you will probably hit your target amount sooner.

2. Choose the type of investment you want

Stocks and shares ISAs have a £20,000 annual limit. Gains are tax-free and so are withdrawals. Lifetime ISAs come with a 25% government bonus on top, however these are for either buying a first home or for topping up your retirement savings, not for other purposes. It's best to use up your ISA allowances when you start investing.

3. Choose a platform, robo-adviser or adviser

This can be tricky as they can all appear to do a similar thing, but think about the range of investments open to you. If you want more choice, then picking a platform that lets you choose your own funds, trusts and shares would be a good shout. If you want someone to do the picking for you, then choosing a platform that selects a portfolio (a ready-made mix) based on your goals and risk profile might make life easier and make you less anxious. A financial planner or adviser will go into the nitty gritty of your circumstances with you and get the right fit of investments for you, but this comes with the highest price tag and if you only have small amounts to start off with, is unlikely to be cost effective.

4. Choose an amount you can afford and consider automation

There is no point investing an amount that takes you into an overdraft every month. Make sure whatever you choose to set aside is affordable. You can always increase your contribution later on. It's also worth considering automating your payment into your investing account – this will make it easier to *set it and forget it* and increase your chances of making investing a habit that you'll keep.

5. Take some risk, but not more than you can tolerate

Choosing a risk approach is always a balance between your growth goals and what you can tolerate – in other words, taking too much risk can make you feel anxious; too little, and your investments might not grow sufficiently to meet your goals. The thing with risk, of course, is that the value of your investments can go down as well as up.

6. Review your investments once a year

Checking in too often can be anxiety inducing, especially if you are a first time investor. Once or twice a year, if you are investing for a long enough time period, should be plenty. ◈

Money
Stories

THREE

"

To get more women comfortable with investing rather than sticking with cash, we need to make it feel more relevant. It's not a question of 'build it and they will come'. If we were all just making rational decisions, then we would all be investing very wisely from a very early age, but that's not how people operate.

IN SEARCH OF GENDER BALANCE IN FINANCE

with Baroness Morrissey DBE

Helena Morrissey

 @HELENAMORRISSEY

 @MORRISSEYHELENA

 30PERCENT
CLUB.ORG

HELENA MORRISSEY *has over three decades' experience in financial services, including 15 years as CEO of Newton. She is lead NED at the Foreign, Commonwealth and Development Office and Chair-designate at AJ Bell, the FTSE250 firm whose mission is to help people to invest.*

*In 2010, Helena founded the 30%
Club. Since then, the representation
of women on FTSE350 boards
has risen from less than 10%
to over 30% and there are now
eighteen 30% Clubs throughout
the world. Helena chairs the
Diversity Project, to improve
diversity across all dimensions in
the investment industry.*

*Helena entered the House of
Lords in September 2020 and was
appointed a dame in 2017. Her
second book* Style and Substance,
*a career guide for women, was
published by Little, Brown Books
on 14th October 2021.*

*Helena is married with nine
children aged between 12 and 29.*

When did you start investing and what was the first investment you made?

Ironically perhaps, given that I was a bond fund manager, my first investment was into property. It was a rollercoaster ride in the earlier 1990s. Interest rates rocketed and my husband and I struggled to make the mortgage payments; neither of us had a well-paid job at the time and we also had a baby before we could really afford it. For a while our outgoings were considerably higher than our income, which was obviously unsustainable. It made me very determined in my career, that's for sure! It also turned out to be a financial opportunity; the value of our small flat plummeted but the cost of a bigger house fell even more and we were eventually able to trade up at what turned out to be the bottom of the market. While that was a great boost, the experience made me wary of property and drove me into the stock market, which was no bad thing.

Can you give us an overview of the state of play with women in UK business and finance?

There's been quite a breakthrough in terms of the numbers of women making it to senior roles in business over the past few years. The shift came first in the boardroom, where we really saw quite remarkable progress in the past decade: the percentage of women on FTSE350 boards rose from less than 10% to over 30% today. Most of that improvement is in non-executive roles. In the last five years progress has finally started to be echoed in senior management positions, with the proportion of female executive committee members and their direct reports now also over 30%. There's still a scarcity of women right at the top, however, with still just 17 female CEOs in the entire FTSE350. And some sectors are lagging, notably the financial sector, where large gender pay gaps show that women are still tending to do less highly valued work i.e., less senior roles than men. I'm convinced that the financial sector is where we should now focus our attention, since it's so important culturally for firms to have women in decision-making roles.

When you first set up the 30% Club, female board membership was around 12.5% in the FTSE100 and 9.5% in the FTSE350. Now that we've made it over the 30% threshold, where do we go from here?

Well, to be honest, I think the 30% target has been perceived more as a shorthand for just wanting better gender balance at all levels. The 30% came about through me realising that it was an important threshold, a point of critical mass. I'm not a scientist or a neuroscientist of course but I'd done a lot of reading around how 30% is the point at which you feel more like a person in the room rather than a token, and that resonated with me. I was the only female member of the Investment Association board for a while, and when I was the only woman in the room – I'm almost ashamed to admit it – I sometimes hesitated from speaking my mind or disagreeing with other people. When you are one of three out of ten, then you're treated like just another person and you feel that way too.

I think it's more important than just raising the target of women on boards. I'm not saying that's won and done, but I think the most important thing is making sure that we have better gender balance and better diversity across all dimensions, not just gender, at *all* levels of companies. Businesses should reflect the customers that they serve and ensure that they don't just have one type of person making it to the top. The global financial crisis came about partly because we had very homogeneous boards, but also arguably because we had group think at the management level as well.

Women are obviously very highly educated these days. It seems such a waste of so much talent that relatively few fulfil their career potential and there's also the argument – particularly relevant when it comes to fund management, I think – around needing more diversity of thought. I don't claim that women are the answer to every aspect of that, but it is a very symbolic starting point for improving diversity of thought.

Focusing in on the financial sector specifically, the median gender pay gap is 28%, which is the largest pay gap of any sector. Do you think the formal mandatory reporting is helping or do we need to explore other measures to combat the gap?

I fear we have lost momentum around gender pay gap reporting, with the 'lost year' in 2020 and now the postponed deadline for 2021 (October rather than April). I've been looking at the trends within fund management specifically, tracking the four years of data that some firms have now released, and we are making some progress but it is slow. The bonus pay gaps are particularly discouraging – women on average receive about half the bonuses of men. Renewed attention around these gender pay gaps and more focus on the actual plans to close them are needed if we are not just going to be wringing our hands for years to come.

I think there is a chicken-and-egg problem. The fact that there aren't many female role models in finance doesn't help. I speak at a lot of schools and universities and very many young girls don't even think of applying because they just think of it as an alien world. They think of it just as a masculine, male-dominated environment, and it is in lots of ways very rational to think that that might prove an uphill struggle compared to if they go to work in a sector that's a bit more balanced to start with. My personal experience though is that being a bit different, even just by being a woman in a man's world can help you stand out and be noticed. In any case, the industry and individual firms need to work harder to attract more women and then ensure that they are included and encouraged in their careers – not simply because that's a good thing to do but because the industry needs to be more balanced, less 'macho'.

Girls are also often put off a career in finance because they think they might need a maths or economics degree to succeed. They don't! I studied philosophy (which has turned out to be surprisingly useful). I'm really trying to encourage companies to ensure they have recruitment policies and criteria that are consistent with their aspiration to attract more women and more diverse talent generally – specifying a "2.1 or higher degree in economics, maths or finance" is just going to put people off.

So, I think there are some practical things firms can do and then as an industry we need to evangelise more and talk about what it is we do. Finance hasn't got a great image and yet in my experience most of those who work within it are simply trying to do a good job for clients and to improve financial wellbeing, which has an important social purpose too. My daughter has just started her first job after graduation working for a company that specialises in investment and advisory work in Africa, another way of both creating value and helping to improve things.

This divide is not just unique to the workplace either, we see it spilling over into personal finance where we see that women are less likely to invest than men are. What do you think the problem is here?

I think that women, when it comes to personal finances, feel that they're not understood, that the language used is either very complicated or very patronising. There are quite subtle differences in what appeals to women compared with men but those can lead to quite different responses when it comes to personal finance. All the studies suggest that women are far more likely to be motivated by specific goals like paying off their mortgage or their children's education than the more general goal of making money – and they are wary of anything they don't quite understand (which is a good trait). I personally hate being sold to – it puts me off completely and I'm confident I'm not alone. We also tend to be risk aware – not necessarily risk averse – but conscious of the risk of losing money, and that tends to make us over-cautious when it comes to investing to grow our money. With interest rates so low and inflation on the rise, that's not a good strategy.

There's a lot of evidence to suggest that women make better investors: what do you think might give women their edge when it comes to investing?

There was a big study in the States with a great title, 'Boys will be Boys', that examined a group of 35,000 American households and their investments. Looking at their returns, researchers realised that the women tended to on average outperform by around 1% a year relative to the men, simply because they traded less. These academics attributed it to the notion that women tend to be less confident than men, and typically overconfidence meant that you tend to act on your beliefs. The problem with over-trading of course is that dealing costs keep eating into returns – and investors also miss out on the big growth stories that take time to unfold.

That spills over, I think, to professional fund management. It sounds almost too stereotypical to be true but I've seen over my long career that women tend to be very conscientious, do a lot of research, be great analysts, consider risks really well and then once they've made their mind up, stick with a position and not trade so much. Now of course the flip side of that is that men are typically (not universally) more decisive, and investors need to have the courage of their convictions, so it's no surprise really that research shows that mixed gender teams perform the best of all.

What advice would you give your younger self or someone looking to start investing?

Like many women, I wish I'd started investing sooner. Good habits can be formed when you are young and I'd tell my younger self to be a little less worried about what might go wrong and realise that putting a little money aside each month and investing in the stock market was a better strategy than trying to time the market. The saying 'time in the market is worth more than timing the market' is good advice.

What can we do to make investing more accessible and appealing to women?

Last year, during lockdown, more of us (both men and women) spent time sorting out our finances, which is a promising start. But to get more women comfortable with investing rather than sticking with cash, we need to make it feel more relevant. It's not a question of 'build it and they will come'. If we were all just making rational decisions, then we would all be investing very wisely from a very early age, but that's not how people operate.

One idea is connecting investing to what it means for our wellbeing, in the way that for example we look after our health. More people these days than ever before exercise and eat sensibly, not because they don't love cake but because they know that in the long term it's not going to be great if they eat lots and lots of cake. We need to get finance into this sense of being an everyday thing. There is also the issue of aligning with values and obviously there is a lot of talk about environmental, social, and governance topics. Climate change or gender equality or just making sure that your money is not financing companies that employ people on zero-hours contracts – these are things that women and young people care about – but they don't necessarily make the connection that they can influence what happens with their money. Making it more obvious that the products and the services that they buy are going to do some good rather than just line the pockets of salespeople would be a step in the right direction.

"

There is no one algorithm
to be successful and the
many different routes
to success come from
diversity of opinions and
ways of doing things.

DIVERSITY: AN ALGORITHM FOR SUCCESS?

with Julia Angeles, Marina Record and Rose Nguyen

🐦 @BAILLIEGIFFORD
🔗 BAILLIEGIFFORD.COM

JULIA ANGELES *joined Baillie Gifford in 2008 and is the portfolio manager of the Health Innovation Strategy. Prior to Baillie Gifford, Julia worked as a management consultant for McKinsey & Co advising firms in Denmark, Russia and Hungary.*

Since joining Baillie Gifford Julia has worked on a number of regional and global investment strategies. Julia has a passion for the transformation taking place in healthcare, and it was this passion which led to the establishment of the strategy. She believes that over the next 10 years healthcare systems around the world will experience a monumental change and we will witness a move away from reactive medicine to a world where prevention and cure will become an integral part of healthcare driven by technology. Julia is also a member of the International Growth portfolio construction group.

Julia obtained a BSc in 1999, MSc in 2001, and PhD in economics from the University of Aarhus, Denmark in 2005. She speaks fluent Russian and Danish.

MARINA RECORD *is a portfolio manager for the Health Innovation team, having joined Baillie Gifford in 2008 as an investment analyst. She worked in a number of global teams before joining Long Term Global Growth, where she focused on analysing companies with the potential for sustained rapid growth. It was here that Marina developed an interest in healthcare, intrigued by the accelerating pace of progress in the field. She joined the Health Innovation team in January 2018 as a portfolio manager, to fully focus her attention on exploring the potential consequences of such progress and how Baillie Gifford can help.*

Marina graduated from the London School of Economics and the Higher School of Economics in Russia with BSc degrees in banking and finance and economics (respectively) in 2008, having studied on these programmes simultaneously.

ROSE NGUYEN *joined Baillie Gifford in 2013*
as an investment analyst. Rose worked on
various regional and global strategies before
joining the Health Innovation team as
a portfolio manager. Having observed
the innovations in multiple industries,
she believes that the great convergence
of different technologies and sciences will
ultimately transform life science. Biology can
move from alchemy and randomness to become a more
predictable, deterministic and repeatable science that will
give rise to a plethora of exciting investment opportunities.
She joined the Health Innovation team in September 2018 at the
inception of the strategy.

Rose graduated BA (Hons) in Economics and MPhil in Finance and
Economics from the University of Cambridge in 2012 and 2013 respectively.

Describe the journey into your role, what attracted you to a career in investment and specifically in the healthcare sector?

Julia: Before choosing economics as a discipline, I considered applying to study medicine. I have always been fascinated by human biology but felt that as my home country emerged from communism, I should study economics. I have always been fascinated with human biology and how little we understand; simple things like how we can treat a disease by taking a pill and it knows exactly what it has to do to address the disease. The more you learn about how medicine works, the more you realise there is such a poor understanding and most of the medicine is very ineffective, with severe side effects. Because I came from Belarus and always thought I would have a career trying to help solve economies in developing countries, that was very naïve thinking in my early 20s. I did a PhD in economics studying financial crises before joining McKinsey for a year and a half as a management consultant. My route into finance was quite serendipitous: investment management never really captured my imagination but after my husband and I moved to Scotland, he suggested that maybe I should reconsider a career in finance. I listened to him and that's when I made the move into finance, but it certainly wasn't my plan from the beginning.

Baillie Gifford really changed my perspective on finance. My association with finance had been with investment banking and I really didn't know much about what fund management involved. The company philosophy at Baillie Gifford was really quite alluring to me because it felt like they're trying to do good things in the context of the industry, so that's why I decided to join.

Marina: I grew up between cultures and countries (Russia, the USA and the UK), and I love that this became part of my identity. Keeping the option to immerse myself into a different culture was an important consideration for me when choosing my education. I found out about London School of Economics' (LSE) external program that would allow me to live and study in Moscow, whilst obtaining a degree that is convertible globally. I was intrigued by economics' combining of psychology and anthropology, and it also meant that I could live in Russia. I always identified as Russian but had not lived there since I was eight, so that's how I found myself in economics.

When I was looking for jobs, investing was one of the careers that appealed to me because it seemed like another way to carry on exploring the world. I hadn't considered Edinburgh specifically, but looked for places where I could continue learning and Baillie Gifford seemed like that sort of environment. I joined initially as an intern for two months and stayed on after my internship finished.

Joining the healthcare innovation team was a natural evolution of my role. I started to come across many innovative companies in healthcare and I wanted to understand what was fueling their progress. Before I knew it, I was spending practically all of my research time looking at healthcare companies.

Rose: I am from Vietnam originally and came to the UK to study when I was 16. I studied economics for a degree, because my uncle who was my role model during my childhood, was a professor of economics in Vietnam. I always looked up to him and I thought I would become a lecturer in economics myself one day, so that was actually my initial plan – to pursue a career in academia.

Towards the end of my master's degree I found that many of the economic theories that I learned from the textbooks seemed a bit out of touch with real life. So I decided that I wanted to find a job in the industry that could allow me to explore how the economy functions. What really attracted me to investing was the potential to positively impact society if you do a good job and allocate resources to companies that deserve it. I started to look into different companies within the investment industry and joined the Baillie Gifford graduate training program, and from there I have been working through various teams within the company. Healthcare was also a natural transition for me. Both of my parents are pharmacists and my partner is a doctor, so I have always been surrounded by conversations about medicine; maybe I evolved into a healthcare investor by osmosis!

There is something that has always fascinated me about different aspects of health, so the health innovation team felt like a natural fit for me to have the opportunity to grow with the team and contribute to the firm and to broader society.

Can you tell us more about the Health Innovation Fund?

Rose: Julia is the founder of the strategy behind Baillie Gifford's healthcare innovation fund. Investing in healthcare is something that the firm has been doing for many years – with more than 20% of the whole firm's assets already invested in healthcare companies.

The pace of innovation in healthcare is accelerating faster than ever before, so we thought that now would be the perfect time to set up a dedicated strategy to invest in this new wave of innovation and to

Actual investors see people's aspirations.

Not assets under management.

BAILLIE GIFFORD | *Actual Investors*

bring together the best companies that are changing human health and healthcare systems in one dedicated fund.

Our strategy is similar to some other strategies that Baillie Gifford has, in the sense that we are looking for extraordinary businesses that can transform healthcare over long investment horizons, 5 to 10 years and beyond. It's the focus and the investment process that sets us apart. Julia has been leading the idea for a few years, but three years ago was when Marina and I joined the team, took that idea and made it into a publicly available fund.

Julia: From my point of view, things really kicked off with the fund when we got together as a team. The portfolio has really been a product of three of us; we all have equal roles to play, because we are all equal decision makers and have the same influence on the strategy.

Comment from Jack Torrance, investment specialist – Health Innovation:

As an observer, the team has three very different personalities which come together like a venn diagram; three different approaches with the sweet spot in the middle.

Julia is the optimist. She has the blue sky thinking – seeing an idea and imagining what it could evolve to be in 10–15 years' time. Rose is more pragmatic, more rooted in the realities of the *now*, asking questions about how we go from A to B, and the steps needed to make it happen. Marina is very systematic and academic in her thinking and ensures that frameworks are applied fairly and we don't get carried away. One thing that is quite unique is the level of honesty within the team. Discussions happen in a very positive way, and it's evident that they are very much three equal decision makers.

Julia: Our team's relationship is one built on trust and trying to do the best job for our clients, but also the investors. As a team, I believe that we're all motivated by the same thing and aligned on what we are trying to achieve. This was quite important in the beginning when the team was about to be formed: we spent quite some time fine tuning the philosophy and making sure we're all on the same page and all agree on the high-level ambitions of the fund.

Marina: There is no one algorithm to be successful and the many different routes to success come from diversity of views and approaches. We inspire each other but we also retain our own personal styles. I think an important cultural quality that we have in the team is our commitment to back each other's enthusiasms. We don't seek a consensus. We explore our different points of view and trust each other not to take challenges personally, but to be open to evolve and learn as we each try to make the best decisions for our clients.

Rose: Having worked in several teams before this, being a young team and also quite a small team makes a big difference, I think our working practices are more flexible and adaptable because we are a younger and more energetic team.

Julia: I think it's also a willingness to experiment and take risks, that again comes from having a younger and more energetic team. We've been experimenting quite a lot and we always want to push and explore the boundaries. Others claim they want to change things but it's what you actually do about it, how radically you're thinking about bringing about that change. I wouldn't say we are too radical but we are trying to continue to challenge ourselves through creativity and innovation.

As an all-female team, do you think there's anything that specifically differentiates you as investors?

Marina: I would say our philosophy is what sets us apart and I don't think it was gender that defined it. We are building something that hasn't been created within our company before and we want to make a difference at an industry level to help companies transform healthcare. Our focus is firmly on the change that we would like to bring and how we can get there. This vision is what unites us.

Julia: Diversity and inclusion have been at the forefront of people's minds now for many years. I think it's less of a question of gender and more about personalities. You can be working in a pure male team, but it's again to what extent has selection bias influenced the team – have the managers who are building the team been choosing those who they are most aligned with, resulting in less cognitive and personal diversity? Equally, you can have a pure male or female team that could display more diversity than a mixed-gender team. When you consider the three of us, although we share the similarity that we studied economics, we are quite different as personalities. It's a very reductionist way to think of diversity based on gender alone.

Are there any challenges that you see in the industry or that you have faced in your own career and do you have any suggestions of how we might overcome these challenges?

Julia: Having a voice and being heard can be more difficult for women in a male-dominated environment. Especially if you're in the minority on your team, it can be difficult to have the confidence to speak up. What I have observed from women I work with, is almost being too much of a perfectionist – they wouldn't speak up unless they're really sure their contribution is adding value whereas men might be more inclined to raise their point anyway.

The other thing is more physiological, when you're stressed out the female voice tends to be higher pitched because your lungs squeeze – this is an involuntary response that you cannot influence. This can become a self-reinforcing negative effect for many women and every time you attempt to speak up, you experience more stress and your voice doesn't come out as you want. Women need to realise it's actually not their fault, it is the responsibility of the whole team to create a comfortable environment to get the best from an individual.

What really changed things for me was the realisation that actually these guys don't know much more than I do and there is still space for me to add value. Then it's a case of working on how you deliver the point you have to make. Your delivery can be improved by meditation and coaching to help you breathe correctly, relax and regain control your voice. Of course, you also have to know your stuff and be sure of that, but once you have control of your physical delivery you should feel less concerned facing these types of situations.

Rose: I agree with Julia's comment, for women it is important to express yourself. From my own experience and from listening to others, something that women tend to do is expect others to read your mind. We should be more proactive and learn to express what we want. For women to feel comfortable doing this it has to come from both sides, whether that's in a relationship or from the organisation you work for, but it's important that it also comes from women themselves.

Marina: Being clear about what I'd like to do in my job and what I need to do the best job I can has helped me tremendously. Then all I had to do was just ask – it's the single most important step in making something possible.

On a different note, I would add that one of the challenges that can hold us back is how we view confidence. I like to see it as humility, being able to listen, to learn and to adjust our views. I was intrigued by how a friend's boss welcomed her into her new role recently. She said: "We pay you for your curiosity and knowledge, not for being right or your desire to win." That kind of statement sets the tone that trickles down into the culture of the organisation.

As we start to see more diversity within teams, how do you think this is going to change the shape of the markets on a global scale?

Julia: If you simply consider diversity in terms of gender, then if you want to counterbalance the lack of diversity within male teams and you bring in some women which provide different qualities I think it's good for the industry. We know from empirical studies that diversity within teams leads to better economic outcomes. With greater diversity we have also seen a big rise in impact investing and quite a few women driving things forwards in this space, suggesting purposeful investment is important to them.

Marina: It's also great that we're starting to explore dimensions beyond broad categories such as gender, for example to include different ways of thinking and backgrounds. There is a huge amount of diversity masked within broad-brushed categories – better understanding of what holds different people back would be a big step toward reducing biases in the availability of opportunities.

What do you feel are the barriers to diversity in finance?

Marina: To benefit from diversity of thought we need to accept people who have experiences that are different from our own. We can't expect people to contribute effectively without making the environment conducive to them expressing themselves. There are likely many layers to doing this well, but as a starting point, we can ask rather than assume. On gender balance, one of the big changes that I'm excited about is equal parental leave. If fully embraced it may still take a generation to really come through, but I think it's a big step toward more balanced gender roles at home and at work.

Is Baillie Gifford doing anything to help encourage people who might be from different backgrounds, or who may not otherwise have considered investing as a career path?

Rose: When I was applying for roles, I compared Baillie Gifford to some other firms in the same industry and what attracted me was that in their description they said that they were looking for someone with an international background – that intrigued me enough to explore things further. Many other companies specify that they want applicants with a quantitative degree in maths, finance, or computer science so it is refreshing that Baillie Gifford is open to people from all sorts of backgrounds. We have team members with degrees from music to geography, history and so on. As a first step this helps increase the diversity of the people that the company recruits, but I think more importantly it's about retaining the diversity and helping create opportunities to encourage those people with different backgrounds to become the leaders of tomorrow.

To really change the work environment and to build an inclusive culture, it has to start from the top, so if you have a leadership team who all think in the same way and have the same backgrounds, they are perhaps more likely to support others who are similar to them. Achieving diversity within the leadership team will filter down to more junior levels and allow the company to retain the diversity. But this will take time, to first hire people from diverse backgrounds and then to nurture those individuals to rise through the ranks and become leaders.

We've touched on some of the traits that have made your team successful; as your team expands, are there any additional traits that you'd look for and are these traits that could be learned and used by retail investors investing their own money or when they are assessing those investing on their behalf?

Marina: I think curiosity is one of the most important traits. It requires the freedom to explore what triggers an interest in us, even if it leads to blind alleys and u-turns. It's the key to new opportunities. That's something we try to nurture and protect within the team.

Julia: It's hard to recommend something that's also relevant for retail investors, but I'd just caution that investment can be perceived as an easy path, but it's not always that way, especially because there are a lot of behavioural biases which can be very hard to control. As a team of professional investors we have the benefit of helping each other to not get carried away with a company by looking out for each other's blind spots.

We generally focus on long-term growth investing, we try to support exceptional businesses for the long term and grow together with those businesses. The evidence suggests a long-term outlook will outperform the short term but also, of course, the culture has to back up the investment style of the company. This is an important consideration for individual investors too; does the approach you're taking with your investments align with your investment philosophy?

Do you have a role model for your careers or do you have coaches or mentors who have helped you, and is there anything that you've learned from them that you would share with others?

Marina: There is a personal definition of happiness that a colleague shared that stayed with me. It is to fully align what we think with what we do and say. I think this is wonderful in its simplicity as a barometer to our choices.

Are there any books that you recommend or that have helped you on your journeys?

Rose: I have read many interesting books related to investment and other aspects of finance, but some of the books that have influenced me most have been outside of that reality. One book that has particularly influenced me is a book called *Harvard Girl* by Liu Yiting, written by a Chinese mum about the journey of her daughter. I read it a long time ago, when I was a teenager in Vietnam and found it very inspiring, so I will say that that's probably one of the books that has greatly influenced me and probably contributed to who I am today.

Marina: *Mindset* by Carol Dweck is a classic, it explores the transitions between a fixed and a growth mindset, with some business and leadership examples of how mindsets can transform the fortunes of organisations and ourselves.

John Cleese's *Creativity* is a fun and short guide to how each of us can set up the best environment for ourselves to tap into a more creative way of thinking. I enjoyed John Kay's narrative in *Obliquity* about why indirect approaches to challenges and goals are usually more effective. On investing, Peter Thiel's *Zero to One* is a great insight into growth investing.

Specifically, on healthcare, this is a little bit more specialist, but I enjoyed *Gene Machine* written by Venki Ramakrishnan, who explores his journey to winning the Nobel Prize. What captured my attention here is how science actually works – the route to breakthroughs is incredibly messy!

Are there any specific technologies or innovations that you're really excited about from an investment point of view?

Marina: What's most exciting is that it's not just any one technology, but many overlapping technologies that are transforming healthcare. Cheaper and more effective tools are expanding our understanding and diagnosis of disease, allowing us to treat the causes and not just the symptoms. A new breed of companies is transforming the pace and chances of success in developing drugs. Sensors and technology are shifting healthcare delivery from hospital visits to remote monitoring and proactive treatment when it's needed – stripping out costs and improving our health. What really excites us as long-term investors is that we can see these changes happening, but we are at a very early stage in all of them. These changes are powered by the creative convergence of science and new technologies – and this creates a powerful window of opportunity for new entrants to redefine the healthcare landscape in the coming decades.

Rose: My favourite is probably quite a common one: companies that are using novel technologies to develop drugs. These new drug classes can potentially change many diseases, but what's more fascinating is that using these novel technologies means companies can potentially develop and discover drugs in a much faster time frame and in a much cheaper and more predictable way than ever before. That can really change the economics of drug development, and ultimately will bring lots of benefits to patients and healthcare systems.

References

Cleese, J. (2020). *Creativity*. Hutchinson.

Dweck, C. (2007). *Mindset*. Ballantine.

Kay, J. (2010) *Obliquity*. Profile Books.

Ramakrishnan, V. (2019). *Gene Machine*. Oneworld.

Thiel, P. (2015). *Zero to One*. Virgin Books.

Yiting, L. (2009). *Harvard Girl*. Writers Publishing House. ◈

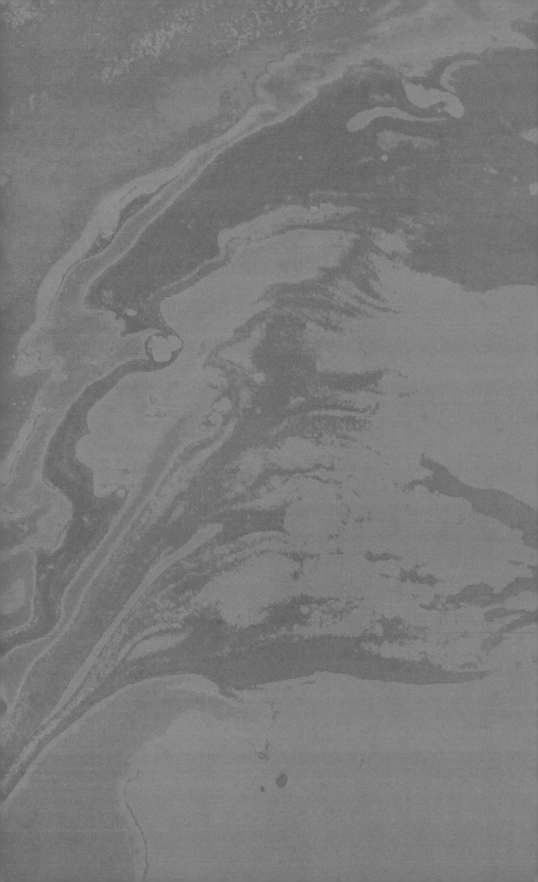

THE VALUE OF ESG INVESTMENTS

with Maria Nazarova-Doyle,
Scottish Widows

Maria Nazarova-Doyle

🐦 @MARIA_N_DOYLE

📍 SCOTTISH WIDOWS.CO.UK

MARIA NAZAROVA-DOYLE
*joined Scottish Widows at the
start of 2020 to lead the customer
investment proposition for the
Pensions business. She is responsible
for defining the investment offering
across all pensions segments
and incorporating responsible
investment principles into Scottish
Widows' investment design.*

> The market turmoil and austere economic outlook which resulted from the Covid-19 outbreak was a true test of responsible investing's resilience and it appears to have passed with flying colours.

Maria holds an MSc in strategic planning and investment from Newcastle University Business School and is a CFA charterholder. She is a member of the PMI Policy Board, CFA UK Pensions Expert Panel, the Taskforce on Pension Scheme Voting Implementation, a spokesperson on investment matters, a regular speaker at DC industry events and a professional awards judge.

C an you tell us about yourself and the journey into your role: why investment?

I have always been fascinated by math and numbers so I found a career in financial services very appealing from early on. I started work in private equity where I had a fantastic hands-on role in valuing companies and figuring out which would be a good investment. I quickly decided that I wanted to contribute to the part of the industry that creates a positive impact on people's lives – and this is how I found pensions. For years now I've been working to help people have better quality of life in their later years by looking after their investments for them. Even though I had provided advice to pension funds on their investment strategies for years, it took some time before I was brave enough to invest for myself. I do wish I'd have come across a book like this back then and I hope that reading about these tips, information and other women's experiences will help you get off the fence and start investing. After all, investing is a long-term game and the sooner you start, the better!

The last year has been a challenging one with the pandemic and many investors have seen their pensions/investments drop in value – what impact have you seen from the pandemic and should we be doing anything to lower our risk?

Covid-19 has not only had a dreadful impact on people's lives, it's driven monetary and fiscal policy, impacted stock markets, influenced trends and changed behaviours.

In March 2020, investment markets saw a dramatic downturn due to the outbreak of the pandemic and the effect that lockdown would have on the economy. The falls in the markets were caused by business-as-usual being disrupted on a global scale, and the fears for the effect it would have on the earnings and share prices of companies across the world. Central banks (such as the Bank of England and the US Federal Reserve) took sweeping actions to pump money back into the system, while governments announced huge relief packages. This helped equities recover. By mid-June, many equity markets around the world had returned to close to where they were before the 'Covid crash' and by the end of 2020 had recovered to deliver positive returns.

It's important to remember that a certain amount of volatility – which is when shares and markets have big sudden swings – is normal, and that a long-term-investment mindset remains crucial. Market reactions are often short-term and emotional, whether based in fear or optimism. Share prices, for that reason, often reflect what professional investors think might happen in the future, rather than what is happening in the moment. That's why it's so important to keep focused on long-term goals, rather than the day-to-day fluctuations in the markets.

A pension is a long-term investment. We know it's difficult seeing your pension and investment values fluctuate. However, as we've seen through previous declines, such as the Global Financial Crisis of 2007–2008, during periods of uncertainty the stock market will drop, but it has also recovered over the long term. Someone who had closed out their investments in March 2020, for example, will have missed out on the market recovery that happened by the end of the year.

There has been one silver lining to have come out of the pandemic – it's making investors more aware of global risks and the need to confront them.

J.P. Morgan asked investment professionals at 50 global institutions how they thought Covid-19 would influence ESG investing. 71% thought it is likely that it will increase global awareness of how a

TAKING ON YOUR FUTURE TOGETHER

Asking the right pension questions now
can make planning for your future easier.
Visit **www.scottishwidows.co.uk**
and we'll help you get started.

high-impact event can affect all our lives and, therefore, will accelerate and increase actions to tackle issues like climate change.

On the face of it, coronavirus and climate change would appear to have little in common. However, as carbon emissions and the push for 'net zero' take centre stage, a number of coronavirus domino effects are providing a helping hand. Biden's election as president has seen the US return to the Paris Climate Accord and target a 30% reduction in emissions by 2030. More than $400bn of the Covid stimulus plan has also been set aside for green spending. Markets are now identifying sustainable investment as a long-term theme, as important as technology and demographics. The push for net zero will impact asset fundamentals and valuations and will be a key consideration for investors in the coming years.

Can you briefly explain ESG/responsible investing and why ESG integration should be a priority for investors in their portfolios?

Global sustainability challenges, such as climate change, inequality, modern slavery and regulatory pressures around these issues are introducing new risk factors for investors. In response, they have been re-evaluating traditional investment approaches.

Responsible investing aims to create a positive impact on the environment, society and the economy, as well as growing investors' money. It is an approach to investment that explicitly acknowledges the relevance of environmental, social and governance (ESG) factors, and of the long-term health and stability of the market as a whole.

Environmental factors may include a company's energy use, waste, pollution, natural resource conservation, and treatment of animals. They can also be used to evaluate any environmental risks a company might face, such as its disposal of hazardous waste, management of emissions or compliance with environmental regulations, and how it is managing those risks.

Social factors examine how a company manages relationships with employees, suppliers, customers, and the communities where it operates. They include workers' rights and working conditions, slavery, child labour, workforce equality and diversity, and health and safety.

Governance factors relate to the rules, practices and codes of behaviour that influence how a company or organisation is run. The quality of a company's governance can have a big impact on its ability to succeed, prosper and survive. It deals with aspects such as a company's leadership, executive pay, audits, internal controls, and shareholder rights.

Responsible investment incorporates this ESG information into investment decisions to help enhance risk-adjusted returns. Known as ESG integration, it's about using non-financial research, data and insights, alongside financial measures, to inform investment decisions.

In short, responsible investing aims to avoid ESG risks and seeks to benefit from ESG opportunities. But why is it important? Not only can this approach result in better investment performance, but it can make a real difference to society and the planet. According to Make My Money Matter, for example, making your pension 'green' is 21 times more effective at cutting your carbon footprint than going vegetarian, stopping flying and switching energy supplier combined.

How is Scottish Widows ensuring it takes a responsible approach to investing?

Scottish Widows' founding mission was to help our customers face an uncertain future. This mission remains as important to us today as it was during the 1800s. We want to help customers invest their money in a sustainable future, meeting the needs of today without compromising tomorrow. We look after the retirement and other long-term savings of millions of people and our role is to help them plan for their long-term financial prosperity. We live in uncertain and challenging times, as we face a staggering array of both social and environmental challenges. Solutions must be found to these challenges to avoid further severe economic impacts.

The events of 2020 have highlighted that the course must be changed to create a society that is sustainable and inclusive, to avoid more serious disruption in the future. To play our part in accelerating this change it's important we continue to use our scale and influence, along with our fund manager partners, to challenge the companies we invest in on our customers' behalf to be the sustainable businesses of the future.

So we're fully embracing responsible investment practices to allow us to manage risks and returns in a more effective way in the funds we offer. It's clear that ESG factors have a financial impact on investments. Companies failing to address ESG issues are likely to see growth severely limited by future regulation, they could be hit with large fines impacting profits and reputations, and they run the risk of becoming out-of-favour with consumers and investors, leading to falls in their value. As well as avoiding the risks, we look to focus on the opportunities, for example companies involved in ESG-positive activities like renewable energy, those managing the transition to a low-carbon economy well, companies with good HR practices and that are well-managed, and those that champion diversity, particularly at board level.

Our approach sees us focusing our investment on companies with strong ESG credentials, engaging with those we believe can do better, and removing the worst offenders we believe can't change.

A slightly contrarian view around ESG investing is that by simply excluding companies who don't have good ESG credentials from our portfolios, we lose our ability to encourage positive change from these companies. What is your view – should we stay invested and use our power as shareholders to instigate change?

Our approach is twofold. Removing all bad performers on ESG factors would mean we lose the opportunity to drive positive change through engaging with those companies. So, we restrict our exclusions to companies that pose the most severe investment risk due to the nature of their businesses and where engagement would make no difference. This includes companies that derive their revenue from thermal coal and tar sands, manufacturers of controversial weapons and violators of the UN Global Compact (UNGC) on human rights, labour, environment and corruption – unless the size and type of investment means that we can influence positive change in their business models.

We also focus our attention on active stewardship. Challenging the companies we invest in to behave more sustainably and responsibly is vital to create sustainable benefits in the long term for customers. We're the stewards of their investments so it's not good enough to leave this crucial activity only to the fund managers we work with. When we have a significant investment in a company and have ESG concerns, we'll always engage with them first. Where we don't see material progress, we'll use our shareholder rights to challenge the company, and will sell our shares where it is clear that progress won't be made.

Where do you focus your investments to enable you to achieve your responsible investment ambitions?

We integrate ESG risks and opportunities into our risk/return expectations when optimising asset allocation. This results in us allocating a significant portion of our investment portfolios to sustainable investment solutions. In 2020, for example, we collaborated with our strategic fund management partner BlackRock, to design an innovative fund which backs businesses that are progressing well in the transition to a low-carbon economy by decreasing carbon emissions, increasing clean technology revenue, and displaying more efficient water and waste management. We're also investing a significant amount in climate solutions such as renewable energy, low-carbon buildings, and energy-efficient technologies.

What do you think is the biggest ESG challenge and what are you doing to address it?

Climate change is one of the biggest issues facing society today and has been recognised by numerous governments as a global emergency. As part of the UK's largest financial services group, we can make a real difference to tackling climate change by helping to finance a greener future together. This will require not only new ways of thinking, living and working – but new ways of investing too.

We know there's an urgent need to transition to a low-carbon future and to grow the green economy, both for the prosperity of the UK and help safeguard our customers' investments and financial futures. Climate change has far-reaching implications in all areas of our lives, including our savings and investments.

This presents us with opportunities to participate in and influence this transition for the long-term benefit of our customers. That's why we're setting ourselves an ambitious goal to decarbonise all our investments by 2050, backing climate solutions and using our engagement and shareholder voting power to drive companies to make the changes necessary within this timescale.

We're committed to gradually reducing the carbon footprint of our investments to net zero. Net zero refers to achieving a balance between the amount of greenhouse gas emissions, like carbon, produced and the amount removed from the atmosphere.

We'll do this by investing in companies adapting their businesses to become carbon neutral and those developing climate solutions, while reducing our investment in high-carbon-emitting companies.

By taking this action, we'll be assisting and incentivising companies we invest in to embark on decarbonisation pathways of a scale and pace needed to prevent global warming exceeding 1.5°C above pre-industrial levels (the objective of the Paris Agreement, an international treaty on climate change).

We're reducing the carbon footprint of our investments to safeguard our customers' savings so that a majority of equities, bonds and property investments will have transitioned to a carbon-neutral position by 2050. The remainder that still have a positive carbon footprint will need to have a credible plan to finish transitioning. And to offset these residual emissions, we'll be increasing investment in climate solutions such as renewable energy, low-carbon buildings and energy-efficient technologies.

But it's important to have shorter-term milestones. We only have a short window to radically reduce emissions – that window closes around 2030. As IPCC research has shown, if we want to hold the line to 1.5°C of pre-industrial levels, we have to cut emissions by approximately 50% by 2030. After that, all signs point to greater levels of greenhouse gases starting a domino effect of climate risks. So our target is to halve the carbon footprint of all our investments by 2030. By 2025, we'll also have invested billions of pounds in climate solutions, such as renewable energy, low-carbon buildings, and energy-efficient technologies. This is a complex undertaking for a provider of our size, but we believe it's essential to set clear milestones to enable us to achieve the 2050 goal.

ESG is becoming increasingly mainstream, do you think in the future that all investments could move towards being considered as ESG investments?

We've seen an exponential growth over the past decade, no doubt spurred on by an increase in evidence that business strategy which takes account of ESG issues results in high-quality management and improved returns.

ESG assets surpassed $35trn in 2020, reaching a third of current total global assets under management, according to the Global Sustainable Investment Association. And according to Bloomberg, global ESG assets are on track to exceed $53 trillion by 2025, representing more than a third of the $140.5 trillion in projected total assets under management.

There's also plenty of evidence that consumers are increasingly interested in the impact their investments are having. A 2020 study from fund manager Schroders highlighted that investors are becoming more likely to put their money where their principles are. It found 77% of investors will not compromise on their personal beliefs when investing, even if that means getting lower returns. Interestingly, it also found 42% of investors are attracted to sustainable investments because they think they are now more likely to offer better returns. Scottish Widows' own research has found that a clear majority of investors want at least some of their pension investments to meet sustainable, responsible criteria.

As individuals how can we be sure that our pensions are being invested responsibly/sustainably?

More certainly needs to be done to help people understand which companies they are invested in – particularly in relation to their pension – and how that is having an impact either positively or negatively on society and the planet. That's why we've created an ESG engagement tool for our workplace pension customers. Among other things, the app shows how the funds someone is investing in, and the companies in which they have the biggest investments, perform against a range of sustainability metrics, both as a simple traffic light score and with a numerical metric. There are similar apps out there in the market where you can check how sustainable your personal investments, ISAs or bank accounts are.

Does a focus on responsible investing compromise the potential returns we might see as investors?

A common argument against investing in assets with ESG criteria has been that they often don't achieve the same high returns as the stocks without this focus. But a slew of research has proved that not to be the case. Numerous academic and investor studies in recent years have found historically lower risk, coupled with outperformance over the medium to long term, for portfolios that integrated key ESG factors alongside rigorous financial analysis

In its seminal research into ESG and financial performance, NYU Stern Center for Sustainable Business uncovered the relationship by aggregating evidence from more than 1,000 studies published between 2015 and 2020.

The researchers found a positive relationship between ESG and financial performance for 58% of the corporate studies focused on operational metrics such as return on equity (considered a measure of a corporation's profitability in relation to stockholders' equity), return on assets (a measure of how efficient a company's management is in generating earnings from their economic resources or assets), or stock price. For investment studies typically focused on risk-adjusted attributes such as the Sharpe ratio, used to help investors understand the return of an investment compared to its risk, 59% showed similar or better performance relative to conventional investment approaches.

Some of the research's key findings included that improved financial performance due to ESG becomes more marked over longer time horizons. ESG investing appears to provide downside protection, especially during a social or economic crisis. Sustainability initiatives at corporations appear to drive better financial performance due to mediating factors such as improved risk management and more innovation, and studies indicate that managing for a low-carbon future improves financial performance.

The market turmoil and austere economic outlook that resulted from the Covid-19 outbreak was a true test of responsible investing's resilience and it appears to have passed with flying colours.

A study by Fidelity International found in the first nine months of 2020 stocks assigned its top rating (A) for sustainability outperformed the MSCI AC World index. It concluded a linear relationship between high ESG ratings and returns over the course of a market collapse and recovery, supporting the view that a company's focus on sustainability is fundamentally indicative of its board and management quality and its resilience. Fund research firm Morningstar showed that its ESG-screened indices largely outperformed in 2020 and over the previous five years, while also offering more downside protection. 75% of its ESG indices beat their broad market equivalents in 2020, while 88% outperformed for the five years through to the end of 2020. And 91% lost less than their market equivalents during the down markets over five years, including the bear market in the first quarter of 2020.

Many ESG-focused funds also beat the overall market amid Covid-19 shutdowns, according to S&P Global. It found that in the first year of the pandemic, funds with environmental, social, and governance criteria outperformed the broader market. S&P's analysis included 26 ESG funds with more than $250 million in assets under management. From 5 March 2020 to 5 March 2021, 19 of the funds grew between 27.3% and 55%, outpacing the S&P 500 index's 27.1% rise, according to S&P. Many other professionals and academics have offered similar analyses that suggest ESG-focused funds and companies were better shielded from the downside of the pandemic.

References

Bloomberg Intelligence (2021). 'ESG assets may hit $53 trillion by 2025, a third of global AUM.' Retrieved from www.bloomberg.com/professional/blog/esg-assets-may-hit-53-trillion-by-2025-a-third-of-global-aum.

Gonçalves, P. (2021). 'ESG assets on track to exceed $50trn by 2025.' Retrieved from www.investmentweek.co.uk/news/4034755/esg-assets-track-exceed-usd50trn-2025.

J.P.Morgan (2020). 'Why COVID-19 Could Prove to be a Major Turning Point for ESG Investing,' Retrieved from www.jpmorgan.com/insights/research/covid-19-esg-investing.

Lefkovitz, D. (2021). 'Morningstar's ESG Indexes Have Outperformed and Protected on the Downside.' Retrieved from www.morningstar.com/insights/2021/02/08/morningstars-esg-indexes-have-outperformed-and-protected-on-the-downside.

Moshinsky, B. (2020). 'Putting sustainability to the test: ESG outperformance and volatilty.' Retrieved from www.fidelityinstitutional.com/en-gb/articles/pages/putting-sustainability-to-the-test-esg-outperformance-903013.

S&P Global Market Intelligence (2021). Retrieved from www.spglobal.com/marketintelligence/en/news-insights/latest-news-headlines/esg-funds-beat-out-s-p-500-in-1st-year-of-covid-19-how-1-fund-shot-to-the-top-63224550.

Schroders (2020). 'Global Investor Study 2020.' Retrieved from www.schroders.com/en/insights/global-investor-study/2020-findings/sustainability.

Take the 21x challenge – Make My Money Matter makemymoneymatter.co.uk/21x.

Whelan, T., Atz, U., Van Holt, T., & Clark, C. (2021). 'ESG and Financial Performance,' Retrieved from www.stern.nyu.edu/sites/default/files/assets/documents/ESG%20Paper%20Aug%202021.pdf. ◈

66

The biggest thing for
all of us to do is to
understand the impacts of
our career choices and
what they could mean for
our futures.

MINDING THE PENSIONS GAP

with Jackie Leiper, Scottish Widows

Jackie Leiper

SCOTTISH WIDOWS.CO.UK

JACKIE LEIPER, *pensions, stockbroking and distribution director at Scottish Widows is a huge advocate of raising awareness of financial resilience, particularly for women. She is an industry-recognised advocate and figurehead for driving societal and political change that will help close the gender pensions gap.*

Jackie is chair of Money Pensions UK's Financial Wellbeing Challenge Group 'Gender and Financial Wellbeing', helping take on the financial gap that exists between men and women, working alongside other key industry figures to make a number of recommendations to help tackle the problem. She is also involved in the Insuring Women's Future initiative sponsored by the CII which focuses on the perils and pitfalls women face when saving for the future. Over the past few years, the programme has investigated the causes of the gender pension gap and has considered the historical and cultural reasons why women can be less financially resilient than their male counterparts.

Can you tell us about yourself and the journey into your role: why investment?

My career has been defined by pensions and investments. I was inspired at Scottish Amicable, when working there as a summer student after leaving school. From there, I held many different roles in frontline operations including heading up and transforming the Prudential's entire telephony operation. I joined Scottish Widows in 2010 to lead the telephony and frontline operations. Subsequently, I have led the multi-proposition distribution teams and have responsibility for the proposition development of our workplace savings, pensions, and investments propositions.

I am hugely passionate about improving financial inclusion, through raising financial awareness and engagement and especially tackling the financial gap that exists between men and women.

Can you give an overview of the state of play with women and pensions in the UK?

There is a significant gender pensions gap which has several underlying drivers but starts with the gender pay gap. The inequalities we see in hourly or annual wages are amplified when looking at the real differences between the pension pots of men and women.

But that's not the whole story. The way in which men and women's career choices diverge at key life decisions, e.g., parenthood or the making/breaking of relationships, contribute significantly to the gap. These structural imbalances mean that women are still saving less than men due to a disproportionate number in part-time or lower-paid work or indeed, taking time out of the workforce to have children. All this combined with the second-highest childcare costs in the world, means UK women are significantly disadvantaged, and it shows up most starkly in their pension pots.

Despite the challenges of the pandemic, the silver lining is that many of us took a renewed interest in our finances. Have you seen a change in behaviour over this period?

Absolutely! People from all walks of life have increased their financial resilience and the pandemic has prompted more people to think about financial advice and their futures beyond the crisis. Our *Retirement Report* shows many people have put the extra disposable income that was reported as a consequence of lockdown to good use, by increasing savings into 'rainy day' funds, paying down debt and mortgages and increasing contributions to pensions. This is great news if it can be sustained, and means that people are more invested in their current and future savings.

Your adequate savings index shows that in 2020, savings between men and women were the closest they've ever been at just 1%, yet the gender pension gap is around £180,000. Can you explain what is driving this gap?

It is very reassuring that the adequate savings index has narrowed to 1% which shows that the automatic enrolment is bringing more people into their workplace pension schemes and has been a key driver and relatively successful. However, given the overall difference in actual savings, there is definitely still more to do to close the gender pensions gap.

Some of this gap is driven by the amount being saved regularly into pensions. For example, women are more likely to be part-time workers or in lower-paid industries which means that they may not hit the auto-enrolment threshold of £10k and may not be aware that they are not contributing to a pension. Women are also more likely to take time out of their career for caring responsibilities or to raise a family which also means lower contributions. The impact is so vast that women would need to work an extra 37 years to have the same as their male counterparts in their pension pots.

What can be done to close this gap, or will it always exist?

We need to be doing all we can to close the gap as it will benefit everyone in society. Since the gender pay gap is one of the big factors contributing to the gender pensions gap, ensuring women have equal career opportunities after education, as well as working with employers to reduce the pay gap will have an effect. Another big contributor to the gap is the unintended consequences of career breaks or reducing working hours, on long-term pension savings. Affordable childcare – to allow both men and women to have fulfilling careers and improved financial resilience, coupled with the shift we are starting to see with more modern family setups where parents share parental responsibilities. In the UK, the nuclear family is still the norm where one parent (usually the woman) takes the higher burden of childcare and household responsibilities.

Improving flexibility, through better maternity and paternity leave options, will allow more women to return to the workforce. Since women are more likely to be in lower-paid or part-time work, dropping the minimum earnings threshold for auto-enrolment, as well as improving communication and education to both men and women on the impact of their career choices on their long-term financial resilience will help close the gap.

Have the increases in auto-enrolment contributions in 2019 helped and will this alone be enough, or do we as individuals need to explore other options to make sure we have enough money during retirement?

The increases are a step in the right direction, but I do worry that many people will assume that this is going to be sufficient for their retirement, whereas we know that people need to be saving at least 12% of their earnings and more if they don't own their own house.

As mentioned earlier, a significant number of people working part time fall under the earnings threshold of £10k and I would recommend, if someone is earning less than £10k, to speak to their employer and opt into their pension.

People who work multiple part-time jobs may also find that they do not hit the minimum earnings threshold in any one of their jobs, even if they earn over £10k in aggregate, and are at a disadvantage.

Starting younger can also help ensure you have enough savings for retirement, however, the current minimum age for auto-enrolment is 22. Younger people should consider opting into their employer pension schemes as well as the benefit of compound interest given the long time they have until they need their long-term savings.

As a guideline, how much should we be investing into our pensions to have a comfortable retirement?

We recommend paying a minimum of 12% of monthly earnings saved into pension pots – this includes employer contributions, and some tax relief too, but also assumes that you will own your house in retirement and will no longer be paying a mortgage or rent. If this is not the case, you need to be saving 15%–20% depending on where you live.

CAN I INVEST MY PENSION
SUSTAINABLY?

For answers to this and the other big questions visit
www.scottishwidows.co.uk

SCOTTISH WIDOWS

Taking on your future together

Most people who want to retire comfortably, would need an annual pension income of around £25k, which includes the State Pension, if you are entitled to it. The current State Pension is just over £9k annually, however it is linked to your employment and specifically your NI record – you need to work for 35 years to achieve the maximum state pension and currently you cannot access this until your mid-late 60s.

I would also recommend keeping track of all your pension pots and considering whether consolidating these would reduce your charges and improve savings, as well as being easier to manage.

Other ways to ensure you have enough in your pension would be to increase your own contributions or to sacrifice any bonuses that you receive as part of your employment.

As well as considering the disparity between pensions for men and women, among women the gap runs deeper with subgroups to consider including younger women, ethnic minorities, mothers, carers, divorced individuals and the self-employed. Do you have any ideas on how we can improve things within these subsets?

There are definitely situations that these subgroups face that disproportionately affect their pensions further. For example, some ethnic minority groups largely rely on one income which means less financial resiliency in the face of income shocks, as we have seen these past 18 months, as well as sole dependency on one pension pot. Policies to support family carers such as providing pension contributions whilst on maternity leave or taking a career break for childcare reasons, as well as cheaper childcare could encourage mothers to return to the workforce and resume contributing to their pensions.

During the pandemic, the government set up the Self-Employment Income Support Scheme (SEISS) to provide support to the self-employed. However, women have been less likely to be eligible and less likely to claim it, which along with the lack of any auto-enrolment mechanism, drives worse outcomes for self-employed women and their retirement preparations. An auto-enrolment system for self-employed people could enable better pensions savings and reduce the gap.

Making the inclusion of pensions in divorce proceedings compulsory as well as retaining pre-maternity contributions for mothers on maternity leave are both policies that could tackle the inequalities some of these groups face.

Is there anything we can do as individuals to rebalance the gender pension gap?

Definitely. Although there are a lot of things that we at Scottish Widows are lobbying the government to change, such as reducing the earnings threshold for auto-enrolment and making childcare more affordable, there are a few things that you can do individually.

Speaking to your employer and opting into your pension, if you do not meet the auto-enrolment criteria, is a good first step. Starting to save into your pension as early as possible really improves the amount in your pension pot and it very quickly adds up.

Keep invested in your personal finances. Often in long-term relationships, the financial wellbeing of the family can end up being one person's responsibility, leaving the partner unaware of their own savings and financial resilience. If the relationship breaks down, remember to keep pensions in the conversations when splitting assets as they're often forgotten, or worse, underestimated which can significantly impact the retirement savings of the person who has been the main child carer.

If you are in employment, ensuring your National Insurance record is kept up to date and that you are paying the correct amount will give eligibility to a state pension. The state pension can contribute significantly to your retirement income, thus reducing the gap.

The biggest thing for all of us to do is to understand the impacts of our career choices and what they could mean for our futures. For example, a career break not only reduces the amount being paid into your employer pension but also your National Insurance contributions, which could affect eligibility for the state pension in the future.

References

Scottish Widows Retirement Report. www.scottishwidowsretirement report.co.uk. 💎

"

Whilst you can't 'personal finance' your way out of poverty, having a basic financial knowledge is something that millions of people lack, and the way we teach children about money in schools is very hit and miss.

FINANCIAL LITERACY AND INCLUSION

with Claer Barrett

Claer Barrett
🐦📷 @CLAERB
▣ FTFLIC.COM

CLAER BARRETT *is consumer editor of the* Financial Times, *and presents the Money Clinic podcast. Claer frequently appears as a commentator on radio and TV, talking about personal finance, consumer and small business issues.*

H ow and when did you get started with investing? Tell us about the first investment you made.

The first investment I made was buying shares in Pearson, the educational publishing company. The reason why? Pearson used to own the *Financial Times*, where I work, and if you were an employee there was a 'share save scheme' where staff could buy shares at a 20% discount. I have always been one for a bargain – if I ever spot a yellow sticker on anything at Waitrose, my eyes light up! So the idea of a discount reeled me in, and then I started asking colleagues questions about how it all worked. If you work for a company that's listed on the stock market, it's likely you will be able to participate in a similar scheme.

Basically, you commit to a set monthly amount that you will save for three or five years (it comes straight out of your pay packet). This could be as little as £5 or as much as £500. At the end of the period, you get the opportunity to buy shares at a 20% discount to the price on the day you started saving. Hopefully you'll get a bargain, and the shares will be worth much more by then – but if they're not, you can get all of your money back – so it's pretty much the closest thing to a risk-free investment. I managed to acquire just over £8,500 worth of Pearson shares when the plan vested, for an investment of £150 a month (so a total outlay of £5,400). I kept them all for a while, and reinvested the dividends into buying more shares. However, I was very worried about having all of my money invested in a single share. In our old office, we used to have a digital notice board in reception displaying the Pearson share price. It was quite depressing coming into work to see that the share price had fallen! So I decided to sell the shares, and reinvest the money in a Vanguard global tracker fund instead, diversifying my investment over thousands of companies all over the world. This proved to be a very wise move, as soon afterwards, Pearson issued an almighty profit warning and the share price fell sharply.

What advice would you give your younger self or someone looking to start investing?

Don't leave it so long! I was 30 before I started – to be fair, I've always been good at saving, and I did buy my first flat when I was 26 (which you could say was a different sort of investment). But even if I'd been able to squirrel £50 every month into a stocks and shares ISA throughout my 20s and 30s, with modest growth assumptions, I'd have an extra £25,000 or so to show for it by now. I look back and think of all of those fifty quids that I probably wasted every month on taxis, dubious fashion choices and boozing in the pub and sigh. With robo advisers and apps like MoneyBox, it's never been easier to quickly set something up and get into the investing habit early on.

What have you learned that has had the biggest impact on your financial success?

Having the confidence to ask for promotions, pay rises and other career opportunities. A lot of women I know work tirelessly hard, and assume that there's some omnipresent all-seeing eye that will magically tally up all this hard work, enter it on a ledger somewhere, and eventually, a pay rise or promotion will land in their lap. This is utter tosh! Make sure that you get the credit for the work that you're doing, and try to think strategically about the projects that you take on at work. For example, I took on the job of organising the 150th anniversary issue of the *Investors Chronicle* magazine (which was a huge amount of work) as it meant I would get to interview lots of *IC* alumni, like Lucy Kellaway at the *FT* and Robert Peston at the BBC. They gave me great interviews about their time on the *IC* and also fantastic careers advice. A few months later, I had landed my dream job on the *Financial Times*!

What would you change to encourage more women to invest their money?

I would love to persuade Tampax, Bodyform and Lillets to have a small reminder on their packaging for tampons and sanitary towels to encourage women into making a regular monthly investment! Our reproductive cycles do give us a big financial disadvantage – you've heard of the gender pay gap, but the gender pensions gap is also a growing problem – and women have longer life expectancies so we need to get cracking earlier with investment to give the money we're able to set aside even longer to compound away. Learning how to invest and manage your money are part of the 'facts of life' in my book.

What are you doing to encourage more equality in finance and investing?

I have helped the *FT* to set up a charity called the Financial Literacy and Inclusion Campaign – *Flic* for short – to spread the message of mastering money far and wide! The pandemic has shown us how precarious people's finances are. We live in an increasingly divided society. Whilst you can't 'personal finance' your way out of poverty, having a basic financial knowledge is something that millions of people lack, and the way we teach children about money in schools is very hit and miss. Young people are a key group that our campaign will target – women and minority groups are two others. These are broad sections of society, but countless studies show that these are the people who face the most disadvantages with their money – and have the most to gain from financial know-how. ◆

DIVERSIFYING YOUR PORTFOLIO

with Claire Dwyer

Claire Dwyer
🐦 @CLAIREDWYER_
◪ FIDELITY.CO.UK

CLAIRE DWYER *began her career in the City after graduating from Oxford University in 2007. She is currently head of Regulatory Solutions at Fidelity International. Last year she was named Rising Star of the Year at the Investment Company of the Year awards. She sits on the Investment Management Examination Panel at the Chartered Institute for Securities & Investment.*

"

Becoming a successful
investor is not an
individual sport. Talk to
people. Pick their brains.
Stay inquisitive, stay
curious, stay focused.

C an you tell us about yourself and the journey into your role: why investment?

There are many appealing aspects of the investment management industry. I suspect the most important, for many of us, is the satisfaction in delighting clients with excellent results. Then there is the continuous intellectual challenge the work provides, as well as its variety.

In the course of my career I have analysed individual stocks, funds, developed entirely new investment products, raised capital and more recently, led a regulatory solutions practice across Asia Pacific, Continental Europe, and the UK.

That blend of the quantitative and qualitative is compelling – and, of course, the relentless questioning of conventional wisdom. In the City you will hear the word *why* a lot.

It is also striking in an industry where so much is intangible, that the consequences of the analysis conducted and decisions taken should dominate every aspect of our lives. Being an investor is a licence to explore the world.

Another point of note is the extent to which the industry has evolved in recent years. The pace of change is extraordinary, exciting and invigorating. Where once the focus was largely on robust financials and technical brilliance, other factors such as environmental, social and governance considerations now dominate boardroom discussions.

Investment trusts have long been an area of interest to you. Why is that?

Investment trusts are arguably one of the greatest innovations of the financial world. The crux of their success is that they've been good at delivering what investors want. The first was launched in 1868 with the aim of giving "the investor of moderate means the same advantages as the large capitalists in diminishing the risk by spreading the investment over a number of stocks." Fast-forward 150 years or so and they are still performing the same function, albeit having exploded in both number and sector reach.

The ability to borrow – or *gearing*, as it is known – has played to the advantage of many of the best-known trusts in delivering superior investment performance. Also appealing to investors is the fact that investment trusts have a fixed number of shares, enabling managers to buy and sell assets at opportune moments rather than being forced to sell in the event of a material number of clients leaving the fund as unit trust managers are required to. Attractive too is the relative stability of the underlying capital base.

A significant feature of any investment trust is its independent board of directors, responsible for safeguarding shareholder interests. Shareholders have the right to vote at annual general meetings (AGMs) and have their say on the re-election of the directors. Increasingly people can attend and vote online, with investment managers looking to promote better engagement. As shares in investment trusts are traded on a stock exchange, like any other listed company, their share price will fluctuate from day to day, reflecting supply and demand.

As a millennial, I suppose I am also swayed by the underlying asset classes, which are often very *now*. Take the Hipgnosis investment trust, for instance, which aims to deliver income and capital growth from investments in songs and associated musical intellectual property rights. Beyoncé, Blondie and Barry Manilow are among the names glittering in the portfolio literature.

How can people use investment trusts in their portfolios?

The first priority in constructing your investment portfolio must be to ensure you are well diversified geographically, between asset classes and, within a country or asset class, between individual investments. The leaders of the pack one year are sometimes the best performers in subsequent years, but sometimes not. It is difficult, impossible even, to predict which way things will go.

Investment trusts can be an invaluable tool in achieving a sufficiently diverse portfolio, by specific exposure to alternative asset classes like property, infrastructure or private equity, for instance. By employing them effectively you may be able to reduce the overall risk of your portfolio, without having to give up too much by way of returns.

Trusts can also be an effective means of adding a new style of investment thinking to your portfolio. You can invest in them via an Individual Savings Account (ISA), a General Investment Account (GIA) or a Self-Invested Personal Pension (SIPP), or indeed for your children or grandchildren by way of a Junior ISA.

What advice would you give to someone looking to start investing?

Becoming a successful investor is not an individual sport. Talk to people. Pick their brains. Stay inquisitive, stay curious, stay focused. The ability to ask the right questions is critical, as well as the facility to find the right building blocks and bolt them together effectively. As with many things in life, the important thing is to actually get started.

On a more practical point, it's never been easier to invest and perhaps, never more important. There is plenty of financial guidance online to be gleaned from reputable investment firms, and companies like Fidelity now even offer an advice service.

A good starting point might be finding out more about where your pension is being invested and following its progress regularly. You might also consider joining a shares club. Also, enjoy the journey, investing has a way of pulling you in!

At what point in someone's life should they start investing?

Ideally as early on as possible but just as importantly, regularly. It is never too late. Investing every month in an ISA is a great discipline which forces you to invest in good times and bad and not to fall foul of the temptation to invest at the top of the market and hold back at the bottom. It's true that choosing investments can be a daunting process, but technology has made things much easier than they used to be and there are lots of useful tools.

How should people go about choosing an investment trust to invest in?

Thorough due diligence is worth the time and effort. How persuasive and robust is the underlying investment strategy? How capable is the manager? When unpicking past performance, ask yourself: what's been the contribution from gearing? How has the discount moved over the last decade, or since launch? How has the trust performed in different market environments? How volatile has the share price and the net asset value been in the last five years? What about the fund manager – what is his or her track record like?

It is also worth looking at the trust in the context of its peers and benchmarks. So also look at board policies on discounts and share buybacks. If you are income focused, what is the trust's history of paying dividends and has the level been sustained? Look at costs. What constitutes a good answer to those questions will depend on your personal circumstances and individual needs.

What investment opportunities or themes are you excited about at the moment?

Much ink has been spilt over whether investing is an art or science. At different points in history it has been markedly one or the other, but in recent years it has been, and continues to be, resolutely both. The landscape of investment opportunities at present is as rich as it is diverse. Among the themes I am most bullish on are artificial intelligence, cloud infrastructure, cybersecurity, digitisation, medical innovation – especially within oncology – disruptive technologies in all their forms, and most of all, climate change.

What would you change to encourage more women to invest their money?

This year Fidelity published its first ever global women and money study. Many aspects of the report make for concerning reading, not least the extent to which women are facing a widening gender pension gap. The study explores the barriers that prevent women from investing, the impact of the pandemic on their personal finances and their approach to retirement planning. It is worth reading if you get a chance.

Among other alarming statistics highlighted, is the fact that two-fifths (42%) of women in the UK don't know how much they have saved for retirement, compared with a quarter of men; that a quarter of women are unsure how much they contribute to their retirement savings each month, compared to 13% of men; and that 13% of women are not making any regular contributions at all to their pensions, compared to 10% of men.

Better support and financial education has to be a key part of this. The financial services industry has a responsibility to get into schools and explain why good financial planning is essential to physical, emotional and mental wellbeing. Let's be less coy about talking about money.

As more women take up leadership roles in finance and investment how do you think this will change the shape of markets on a global scale?

At Fidelity we are already enjoying the fruits of having two exceptional women as our Chair and Chief Executive Officer. Better representation of historically under-represented groups is something we will see more of in the years ahead. Two things are very striking about how the diversity conversation is evolving. The first, the degree of interest from regulators and the second, the extent to which we've got better at thinking about diversity in the broadest sense, encompassing areas like neurodiversity as well as the more traditional diversity categories.

In a recent discussion paper, the UK regulator, the FCA, set out a number of policy options including, among others, the use of targets for representation, measures to make senior leaders directly accountable for diversity and inclusion in their firms, linking remuneration to diversity and inclusion metrics, as well as considering diversity and inclusion in non-financial misconduct. Data and disclosure will be key and will inevitably shape the way business is done.

What traits do you think give an investor the edge in their investing? Do you think women have any traits that can be considered to be a secret weapon when it comes to investing?

I'm reluctant to label specific traits as masculine or feminine, as I often see greater differences within genders than between them, but it's very clear to me that the best investors are both disciplined and energetic. They tend to be people who can both trust and challenge their intuition. They are bold and willing to venture into the unknown, in the full knowledge that success is never guaranteed.

Good investors are good listeners, hard workers and intellectually curious. They are realistic about expectations, with the ability to be self-critical and self-questioning. If they are confident, it is well-calibrated confidence. Ultimately, the capacity to be patient is critical to success.

References

Fidelity Global Women and Money Study. Retrieved from www.fidelity.co.uk/women-and-money/global-women-and-money-study.

Foreign and Colonial Government Trust, 1868. ♦

MAKING MONEY MAINSTREAM

with Kalpana Fitzpatrick

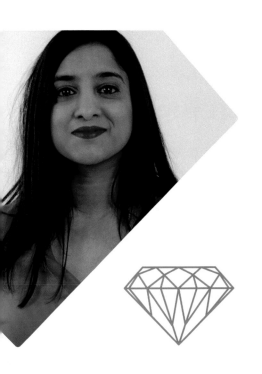

Kalpana Fitzpatrick

🐦 📷 @KALPANAFITZ

◩ THEMONEYEDIT.COM

KALPANA *is an award-winning journalist who has worked for a number of high-profile media outlets, including national papers and women's magazines. She is currently the editor of The Money Edit, recently launched by Future Plc.*

"

Our desire to research
and think carefully about
what we are doing – and
then sticking to our guns –
is our secret weapon.

Prior to this, Kalpana was finance editor for a portfolio of women's lifestyle titles at Hearst UK, which includes Cosmopolitan, Good Housekeeping, Red *and* Prima. *Kalpana played a pivotal role in launching money content into these titles, to help women with their personal finances.*

She started her career at the Financial Times Group, covering pensions and investments.

As a money expert, Kalpana is a regular guest on TV and radio. She is also the resident money expert for the BBC Money 101 podcast and co-author of the e-careers personal finance course.

Kalpana is passionate about helping people be better with their money, and in particular, helping women who have never invested to get started.

How and when did you get started with investing? Tell us about the first investment you made.

Before I went backpacking in 2004, I decided to put some money into savings because I didn't want to return skint. Not really knowing what I was doing back then, I walked into Nationwide Building Society and put £2k into an ISA index tracker fund.

I haven't touched that money since that day, and it has pretty much tripled in value. I've left it there to continue growing.

This, you could say, was the start of my investment journey. I now make use of my ISA allowance every year when I can, knowing my money is working hard for me.

What advice would you give your younger self or someone looking to start investing?

Start as soon as possible. I have always been a good saver, but I didn't invest because no one told me about it.

I had a Saturday job working in a shoe shop when I was 16, and I used some of my earnings to buy clothes and stuff and then put some of it into cash savings. I wish someone had told me to invest it instead. Sadly, the only investment I heard people talk about was to purchase a buy-to-let property! On that note, I would say, don't follow the hype, or fashionable trends, just because friends, family, influencers and strangers at the bar are talking about it. Whether that is property, cryptocurrency or stocks in certain companies.

Do your own research. A lot of investment companies have resources on their sites – use them. There are many journalists like myself who are always educating their readers, and then there are also some great books out there too. Educate yourself and then make decisions that you feel comfortable with and fully understand.

Is there anything you would do differently with regard to your investment journey?

I really believe investing is one of those things that you don't know how lucrative it can be when it comes to building wealth until you actually do it. And sometimes, overthinking it before you get started can be a barrier – just do it. I am glad I walked into Nationwide that day and naïvely put money into a ISA. If I spent too long thinking about it, I may never have done it.

What is your best, favourite or most worthwhile investment?

It would have to be that very first ISA I opened before my backpacking journey. But now, I also pick my own funds, and currently one of my best funds happens to be 'global agriculture' followed by a 'positive change' one.

What are the one to three books that have greatly influenced your investing/financial journey?

I tend to read *MoneyWeek* magazine, but I will dip into books for inspiration to do better and to do more. One of my biggest inspirations has been *Rich Dad, Poor Dad* by Robert Kiyosaki – which really makes me think about how important it is to build financial intelligence and I like the message that you do not need to be a high earner to be rich.

I Will Teach you to be Rich by Ramit Sethi is another of my favourites – I love his messaging that we need to stop worrying about whether we can afford that latte, but to instead focus on the big wins, ways to save large amounts of money that genuinely make a difference to your life – like investing.

What do you think the biggest barrier is for women investing?

There are so many, but it's certainly a lack of role models, which results in investment companies not connecting with women.

Morningstar research found that there are more funds run by men called Dave than there are run by women. And when Morningstar looked at 1,496 UK-listed funds, 105 of those were run by women. Out of almost 16,000 active fund managers globally, only 1,725 are women.

So, we need to see these companies open up to women and encourage more diversity, because so far, we only have one side of the story.

It's also important to understand that there are many myths around investing that stop women from taking the plunge. Many people I speak to see investing akin to gambling, they think they have to have a lot of money, or they believe that they will lose money if they invest and so it is safer in cash. Some people believe it's all about stock picking, when actually, digital providers make it a simple process where you can start investing by answering a few questions based on your attitude to risk, and often with just a small amount of money.

There is a real lack of financial education, so the more we talk about investing to help people understand it, the better.

What would you change to encourage more women to invest their money?

I'd like to see investment companies ban the jargon and stop with the macho images on their websites/brochures.

What are you doing to encourage more equality in finance and investing?

As a journalist, I have a platform that gives me the opportunity to build the narrative around closing the investing gap.

Until recently, I was finance editor for a portfolio of some of the UK's top magazines, where my aim was to help launch finance content into a number of brands. This included talking to readers about investing; I made sure articles were relatable, jargon free, and inspiring with real life stories.

Now, as editor of a new money site (TheMoneyEdit.com), I am on a mission to educate everyone about their finances, including investing and building wealth.

I also regularly talk about investing on my Instagram, where my followers are really interested in how to get started.

Do you think women have traits which give them an edge in investing? What trait(s) do you consider to be the secret weapon?

Although fewer women invest, when they do, they do it better than men. That's because they invest and hold, and they don't make hasty decisions. Our desire to research and think carefully about what we are doing – and then sticking to our guns – is our secret weapon.

What have you learned that has had the biggest impact on your financial success?

I really value my time and there's a good reason why they say 'time is money.' You can waste so much time trying to save small amounts of money or moving money around from one account to another. I automate as much of my finances as possible i.e., standing orders that pay directly into an ISA each month, using direct debits for bills, but also not spending a lot of time moving my investments around. Value your time if you value your money.

What investment opportunities or themes are you excited about at the moment?

Probably green investments, because I know my money has the power to help save the planet. Emerging markets is another area I am keen on – I've been investing in these markets for years and they are always good ones to keep your eye on.

Can you share a story about the one that got away – an investment opportunity that you passed on that went on to grow beyond your expectations?

I can't think of any one opportunity that I wished I had grabbed, because let's face it, there are loads of things you end up knowing about when it is too late. But I do wish I was more active with my children's Junior ISA sooner and had a wider selection of funds in their portfolio – but I won't beat myself up about it as we were sleep-deprived parents.

Is there anything else you would like to share to inspire others? A favourite quote, investor role model or anything else?

I'm a massive fan of Warren Buffett. My favourite quote from him is 'Only when the tide goes out do you discover who is swimming naked.'

The one I live by: 'The most important investment you can make is in yourself.'

References

Esposito, A. (2019). 'More Funds Run by Daves than Women.' Retrieved from www.morningstar.co.uk/uk/news/197122/more-funds-run-by-daves-than-women.aspx.

Kiyosaki, R. T. (2000). *Rich Dad, Poor Dad*. Warner Books.

Sethi, R. (2010). *I Will Teach you to be Rich*. Yellow Kite. ◈

CLOSING THE ETHNICITY INVESTMENT GAP

with Selina Flavius

Selina Flavius
@BLACKGIRLFINANCEUK
BLACKGIRL
FINANCE.CO.UK

SELINA FLAVIUS *is the founder of financial coaching company Black Girl Finance. She also hosts a weekly podcast of the same name, and is the author of the book* Black Girl Finance: Let's Talk Money *and creator of the Black Girl Finance Festival.*

"

Investing alongside
equal pay, are the two
things that will bridge
the wealth gap that exists
for people from BAME
backgrounds.

Selina is on a mission to make money conversations more inclusive and recently won a British bank award for financial influencer of the year. After a 15-year career in business development, she decided to follow her passion for finance and launch Black Girl Finance as a safe space for women with a massive focus on Black women and women of colour to talk about money. She has also contributed to discussions in the UK media about financial inequality, and worked as a contributor to the Money and Pensions Service's 10-year UK Strategy for Financial Wellbeing.

How and when did you get started with investing? Tell us about the first investment you made?

Some of my very first investment opportunities came through working. The first time was when I was auto-enrolled into my employee pension scheme, when auto-enrolment was first introduced. Prior to this point, I had wanted to invest, but was not sure how to get started. I knew I needed a pension so I didn't opt-out and my pension was invested through Aviva. The second time was again facilitated through work, when the company I worked for was acquired by another listed company and I was offered the opportunity to invest through a company salary sacrifice discounted shares scheme. We put money aside every month for six months and then our company shares were purchased at the lowest price over the previous six-month period. So effectively at a discount to the current stock market price. These are both examples of investing in a passive way but not really being in control of what I invested in.

When it comes to me actively making an investment choice, I was a massive fan of Warren Buffett's approach to investing – dollar-cost averaging and diversification through index funds. So I made the decision to invest in a FTSE 100 index fund through Hargreaves Lansdown. This was the very first investment I made of my own choosing and I felt very proud to finally have taken the bull by the horns and started my investing journey.

What advice would you give your younger self or someone looking to start investing?

My advice would be that it's never too early to start investing and it has never been cheaper or easier to begin and learn. The amount needed to begin investing is extremely low due to the fintech apps we have on our smartphones. There are numerous options available if you want to get started investing whilst learning about investing at the same time. You can use a round-up app such as Moneybox, or robo adviser app such as Wealthify, or invest in an index fund. All are great options to start investing with small amounts of capital and you don't have to decide where you invest in the case of Moneybox or Wealthify; the funds are picked for you. Whilst you make these small investments, you can observe and learn how your investments are reacting and changing, as the local economy changes, as the global economy changes, or as the sector you are investing in changes. The global pandemic being a recent example comes to mind, and as someone who decided to invest a little in China prior to everything happening over there, it has been a really interesting learning curve. It's an invaluable investing experience seeing one market doing really well whilst another is depressed, and being invested in both – it stresses the importance of diversification and truly allows you to understand your risk appetite. Through actually taking the plunge to invest you learn so much.

Is there anything you would do differently with regard to your investment journey?

Yes, absolutely! I regret not starting investing sooner. I was working for roughly eight years before I started investing. Having worked through and after the 2008 recession, I think about all the stock market gains I would have made since then, all of the compound interest

I missed out on by not starting earlier. Another thing I would have done differently was made sure I invested in a stocks and shares ISA: having investment in a general investment account subject to capital gains tax, when there is a way to not pay capital gains tax on my initial investments, was a bit of a beginner faux pas. Thinking about ways to invest in a tax-efficient way is an important consideration. Anything that cuts into how much of our investment we can keep, whether it be fees or taxes, should be taken into account. I didn't know this when I first started out.

What are the one to three books that have greatly influenced your investing/financial journey?

A book about investing that I listened to and read numerous times was *The Intelligent Investor* by Benjamin Graham. It's not the easiest book to read and it can feel very dated because it is very old. But the principles about investing were there, and it is why I started investing in index funds in the first place. Another book I read about investing was *One Up on Wall Street* by Peter Lynch. It's been a very useful book for learning strategies to pick individual companies to invest in. Both books have been invaluable in providing clear strategies to invest.

What are you doing to encourage more equality in finance and investing?

Through my platform Black Girl Finance, I ensure that finance is a topic of conversation for women who are from a similar background to myself, black women and women of colour, I point them towards useful resources and support to bolster financial wellbeing. I also ensure that investing is front and centre of the conversation. We run regular online webinars called the Black Girl Finance Festival. Which is a day-long event, the last event was focused solely on investing. In the current climate of low-interest rates on savings, high rates of inflation and the financial education gaps that exist, I will keep having these conversations and providing events because investing alongside equal pay, are the two things that will bridge the wealth gap that exists for people from BAME backgrounds. The events are also an opportunity to showcase black women and women of colour who work in finance. It's about highlighting the incredibly diverse women working in finance, and inspiring the next generation into the field.

References

Graham, B. (1973). *The Intelligent Investor.* HarperBusiness.

Lynch, P. (1989). *One up on Wall Street.* Simon & Schuster.

THE FINANCIAL EDUCATION REVOLUTION

with Vivi Friedgut

Vivi Friedgut

🐦 @VIVIFRIEDGUT

🔲 BLACKBULLION.COM

VIVI FRIEDGUT *is an Australian fintech entrepreneur based in London. She is the founder and CEO of Blackbullion, the financial wellbeing brand for Gen Z which supports over 500,000 students across dozens of universities and colleges in the UK, Australia, New Zealand, Ireland and South Africa.*

"

I believe that education needs to be paired with action and that we need to demystify the language and encourage people to think more about how they want their lives to look and how their money contributes to this vision.

Vivi is a former wealth manager, an author and media commentator who is obsessed with the power of fintech to tackle one of the greatest global challenges – *financial illiteracy and the impact this has on long-term indebtedness, inequality and future financial freedom.*

How and when did you get started with investing? Tell us about the first investment you made.

I am really lucky because I was raised by parents who believed (and continue to believe) in the importance of financial education. From an early age they did all they could to involve me, and my brothers, in all sorts of financial decisions and discussions in order to raise our confidence. I actually turned a lot of these lessons into a book (my first) – as I maintain that the best way to learn about money is through discussions and role models. It's only years later that you realise how lucky you were to have conquered some of the fears around complex matters, like investments, early. I actually made my first foray into the stock market when I was 15 years old and bought a small parcel of bank shares. Of course I wasn't old enough to do it myself and my mum bought the parcel on my behalf. I caught the bug early and used to check the papers every day (no apps back then). I was totally hooked.

What is your best, favourite or most worthwhile investment?

As things stand right now my best, favourite *and* most worthwhile investment is my apartment. I've always been a good little saver and have worked in relatively high-earning professions (until I started my own business and my salary practically returned to what I was earning in my early days working shifts at McDonald's!) I got a good deposit together from those years of squirrelling away every penny I could and got really lucky that the moment I got enough money together for a decent-sized deposit, and found a place I liked, was also the week the property market began reversing from its downward trend. The bottom of the financial crisis was when buying a property was last 'affordable'. I was also one of the few people to benefit from the first-time home buyers' stamp duty boost. We were due to complete the day of the budget and my conveyancer suggested we postpone completion by 24 hours because of the rumour mill, which turned out to be true. In the 10 years I've lived in this apartment it's probably earnt more than I have and the value has almost doubled. I'm very much hoping that in the coming years this answer will change and my new answer will be "investing in my business." On paper this is where the majority of my net wealth currently lies and my hope is that quitting the corporate world and building Blackbullion will have turned out to be not just my greatest career move but a terrific financial move as well.

What do you think the biggest barrier is for women investing?

By and large I hate the cliche about female investing but unfortunately like so many cliches it's a cliche for a reason. That cliche is that women seem to lack confidence when it comes to investing. We see time and time again when we speak to male students their eagerness to get into investing and crypto while female students seem a bit more hesitant. I am not a psychologist and I am sure there are millions of words written on this subject but this is the anecdotal evidence. This nervousness is by far the biggest barrier. One of the greatest advantages of learning about investing and the power of the financial system young, is that when you are young you have a much lower fear reflex. You're more likely to give something a go because your ability to assess and analyse risk (and the potential outcome of those risks) is much lower. Of course this can have terrible consequences too! The older we get the more fearful we become about the unknown, and investing is seen as a more scary financial activity. It feels far less anxiety-inducing to put money into a cash ISA than it is to put money into the stock market. Unfortunately the financial rewards reflect this behaviour. Many others address this question by speaking about the fact that the investment world is geared more towards men, advisers are more likely to be male – both of these are (again anecdotally in my experience) true and evidenced in the years I worked in wealth management surrounded by male advisers and male clients. I believe these create higher barriers to women participating fully, but am not convinced that they are the biggest factor. Others I am sure will disagree.

What would you change to encourage more women to invest their money?

I think it's terrific that there are women and companies specifically focused on helping women to invest their money and consider more broadly their financial circumstances. But I also feel that sometimes these focus a lot on stereotypical female issues and will perpetuate stereotypes. The only advice I have, is, I believe the only advice that makes sense: that women need to dive into the water. Start small, but start! The only way to get comfortable in this crazy ocean we call the investment world is to put a small amount of money in and learn as you go. My recommendation to people is always to pick a stock or a fund or some other asset and watch it. Get comfortable with the fluctuations, understand market movements and what influences them and then put some money in. Just like sport, there is only so much you can do without getting into the game. You can't get good at kicking a football by watching YouTube and reading books – when it comes to financial training the best learning is in the market itself. Put in a small amount of money – my first investment was $200 as a teenager (and today you can start even smaller) – but get into the game because the only way to build confidence is to play.

What are you doing to encourage more equality in finance and investing?

I feel so strongly about the fact that more people should be investing, building their wealth and considering money as a vehicle towards personal freedom that I started a business centred on this mission. I believe that education needs to be paired with action and that we need to demystify the language and encourage people to think more about how they want their lives to look and how their money contributes to this vision. We need to be honest about that avocado toast, we need to be honest about the fact that you can only spend money once, and we need to be honest that women have far more control over their personal finances than we give ourselves credit for. Governments will regulate and companies will try to sell goods and services but it is for individuals (especially today) to decide how to respond. There is a statistic I saw when I first started the business out of the United States which was that for every $1 spent on financial education, $25 was spent on promoting financial products. That's a shockingly difficult mountain to overcome, but we also need to be honest that Kim Kardashian buys something and it sells out, Kate Middleton dresses her kids in something and it immediately sells out. We have power over our spending and financial behaviour and while we are absolutely bombarded by pressure we need to acknowledge that peer pressure is not new. As a sector, financial services need to create better products and we can all help empower individuals. In essence this is what Blackbullion is all about and I hope that we can 'slowly and then quickly' influence the decision making of young people all over the world toward money being a vehicle for financial freedom, not a vehicle towards accumulating more tat!

What investment opportunities or themes are you excited about at the moment?

I'm particularly interested in the growth of ESG as an investment category. Historically, *impact* has been a word used with some contempt as opposed to representing companies seeking an outstanding commercial opportunity whilst tackling a major societal challenge. But I believe this is changing fast as we turn our heads more towards sustainability and using our money as a way to signal the kind of moral and ethical changes we want to see in our world. I'm also very excited about the number of young businesses that are starting to grow in fields that have long been neglected, like healthcare, education, femtech and the environment. It is a fact that where money goes, creativity flows, and at the moment a lot of money is seeking placement which is fuelling businesses that might not be able to access funding usually. I'm also very excited about the opportunities presented by a post-Covid world – from reimagining workplaces to cities to transport; the pandemic has brought about a revolution in how people think about their day-to-day life and also how they spend, and where they spend their days. This will have inevitable consequences on everything from our high street to our high schools and – while all change is terrifying – we have an opportunity to create the world that we want, if we are only smart enough to grab the opportunity. After all, a crisis is a terrible thing to waste!

Can you share a story about the one that got away – an investment opportunity that you passed on that went on to grow beyond your expectations?

I desperately try not to look backwards and regret decisions, because there is no positive energy that comes from doing that. That said, the investment opportunity that I passed on and regret is not purchasing an apartment in Melbourne Australia when I lived there for 12 months before moving to London. My boss was going to buy an apartment in an area called Richmond, which at the time was up and coming, and told me there was an apartment next door also being sold and that I should buy it. I said no – I didn't know what I wanted to do with my life and this was too much of a commitment. The apartment has probably increased in value by a factor of at least 10 since then and I would've made a very significant profit! But I don't spend a lot of time regretting that decision, because the trajectory of my life would've likely been very different had I laid down property roots in Melbourne. I may never have left Melbourne, let alone Australia, and would never have had the opportunities that I've had, both personally and professionally since moving to the UK. While there is no real regret, I did learn a critical lesson – make financial decisions based on the quality of the asset in play and not personal circumstances. 20 years ago it would've been hard to imagine just how small the world was going to become, and how mobile. Today I would like to think that is an opportunity that I would not pass on if it came up again.

"

The moment you invest
once and realise you
won't lose *all* your
money and that you don't
need a *lot* of money to
invest, it all changes!
The fear dissipates and
excitement ensues!

BREAKING DOWN BARRIERS IN INVESTING

with Prerna Khemlani

Prerna Khemlani

@THISGIRLINVESTS

THISGIRL
INVESTS.CO.UK

PRERNA KHEMLANI *is a qualified chartered accountant, a finance manager at Coca-Cola Europacific Partners and a One Young World ambassador. She is also the founder of This Girl Invests which has been featured on* Glamour UK *and* Cosmopolitan UK.

This Girl Invests' mission is to help reduce the gender investment gap by using education as a tool to empower women to invest and to feel #financiallyconfident. This is achieved by creating easy to understand (jargon free) personal finance & investment content, online courses and webinars.

Prerna also raises awareness by delivering corporate and university talks to a wide range of investors. A few client examples include multinational Swiss pharmaceutical Roche, UC Santa Barbara, and The Junior League of Charlotte.

How and when did you get started with investing? Tell us about the first investment you made.

I knew there had to be a better way to manage my money when my salary was increasing but I still didn't feel like I was earning more – I know now this is lifestyle creep! This is when I realised that investing didn't require a lot of money – the goal is simply to buy assets that will grow in value over time. At the time, I was in my first graduate job so I had to look for a way of investing that worked for me and that's when I discovered Moneybox – which rounded up every time I spent money – that was the first time I dipped my toes into the investing world. Frankly, the moment you invest once and realise you won't lose *all* your money and that you don't need *a lot* of money to invest, it all changes! The fear dissipates and excitement ensues!

What advice would you give your younger self or someone looking to start investing?

Speak to people – it feels taboo to talk about money but I have learnt so much from conversations with friends and family. If not that, listen to podcasts, read books – start to take an active interest in knowing how to manage money. It is certainly one of the most useful life skills I've learnt.

What are the one to three books that have greatly influenced your investing/financial journey?

The Meaningful Money Handbook by Pete Matthew

The Simple Path to Wealth by J.L. Collins

The Richest Man in Babylon by George S. Clason

What are you doing to encourage more equality in finance and investing?

I've founded an online community for women called This Girl Invests – we provide corporate talks, hour-long masterclasses on all topics from budgeting to property investing, a month-long introduction to money called 'The Money Transformation Program' and one-to-one coaching services. All without the jargon!

I believe that creating a safe space where women can ask any question without wondering if it's a stupid question leads to some wonderful conversations on money, financial wellness and investing!

What investment opportunities or themes are you excited about at the moment?

I find the world of personalised medicine and medtech exciting. With the advancement of technology and speed of data analytics this will certainly be a space to watch!

Do you think women have traits which give them an edge in investing? What trait(s) do you consider to be the secret weapon?

Women are known to be risk averse – this really just means we are more likely to buy and hold than to trade. This, of course, leads to higher returns and less transactional costs. I think our secret weapon is research – we like to know what we're getting ourselves into and this is very important in investing! Doing the due diligence before investing is crucial!

References

Clason, G. S. (1926). *The Richest Man in Babylon.* Penguin.

Collins, J. L. (2016). *The Simple Path to Wealth.* CreateSpace.

Matthew, P. (2018). *The Meaningful Money Handbook.* Harriman House.

IMPROVING FINANCIAL WELLBEING

with Laura Pomfret

Laura Pomfret

🐦 THEFINANCIELLE

📷 @FINANCIELLE

◪ FINANCIELLE
.CO.UK

LAURA *is founder of Financielle, a female-focused financial wellness brand empowering women to take control of their money and build dream lives. The Financielle Playbook and app have helped thousands of people to ditch debt, build savings and grow investments.*

"

When I started to focus
on financial wellness
rather than wealth,
things started to change
massively. Being in
control of money, being
stable and building
financial security for
the future is the most
empowering thing anyone
can do for themselves.

Laura has a vision to close the gender wealth gap by focusing on financial education and the benefit of community to support women to build strong financial futures.

Ⓗ ow and when did you get started with investing? Tell us about the first investment you made.

I was the worst investor to start off with – in my early twenties I actually opted out of pension contributions, with the view that I would start them again when I earned more money. Money was tight and no one in my family or peer group had the knowledge to say that this was crazy.

Whilst I did then later start contributing to my pension again, I still didn't see this as investing. As I embarked on a financial education journey, the penny dropped and I immediately ramped up contributions and opened my very first stocks and shares ISA, probably around 10 years ago now, and I've never looked back.

What advice would you give your younger self or someone looking to start investing?

Too often when we're young it's easy to put things off until later, waiting for a time when we've more money or more time. The biggest mistake we can make as younger investors is putting off investing until later as we miss out on the golden early years to get compound interest ticking.

It's also a massive habit-builder, treating investing as natural as paying for your mortgage or your utility bills. If you always treat it as a given that investing is in your budget, you then have the benefit of a strategy over willpower i.e., remembering to invest.

What is your best, favourite or most worthwhile investment?

Investing in a whole-of-market fund with the benefit of a pension wrapper was an absolute game changer. Going from tiny contributions to chunky ones, the employer contribution, the government tax contribution and seeing all that tracking the market really blew my mind. So simple, requiring very little market knowledge, just invest and leave.

What are the one to three books that have greatly influenced your investing/financial journey?

I've been more influenced by blogs such as Mr Money Moustache and Financial Samurai from the US, teaching me about the concept of financial independence; plus I was really encouraged by the community feel in the early forum days of Money Saving Expert in the 2000s. Although American, *Rich Dad Poor Dad* by Robert Kiyosaki helped me to understand that it is important to not just rely on a salary for the rest of my life and to start looking at building assets that grow and also provide diversified income streams. This was what inspired me to buy my first rental property and to later ramp up my investing in the markets – purely due to the principle that we shouldn't just exchange our time for money alone.

What do you think the biggest barrier is for women investing?

The majority of financial products are built by men, for men. They don't speak to women. Women want to know the context and wider implications of financial decisions before they take the leap; it's a bigger picture rather than an isolated decision and I think this is reflected in many areas of life as a woman.

Secondly, and crucially, women typically have less money than men to invest. We are already statistically likely to be paid less due to the gender pay gap and we are aggressively targeted by brands to spend our money on products to make us look better aesthetically, rather than direct money into products that will help it grow.

I think another barrier is lack of community when it comes to investing. We need to talk about money and those who invest need to share their stories and experiences to help inspire the next wave of female investors.

What would you change to encourage more women to invest their money?

We need to see female-focused investment brands and this was why we decided to build Financielle – a brand that creates a safe space for women to learn about their finances and walks with them on their money journey, through various stages until they have the confidence to invest and grow wealth for their future.

Do you think women have traits which give them an edge in investing? What trait(s) do you consider to be the secret weapon?

Yes, I believe because women want to understand the wider context of their financial decision – how it fits in with their own financial life and in context to wider society, they are more likely to make sound investment decisions. I also think women tend to be more purpose-driven than men when it comes to their consumer habits and we see the same within our community when it comes to investing too. Purpose-driven companies are having their moment in economic history and are likely to for some time to come – meaning investments in them, particularly ESG investments, will likely do well.

What have you learned that has had the biggest impact on your financial success?

I had a lightbulb moment in my twenties where I realised that the system was stacked against those without financial literacy. Society is obsessed with consumption, keeping up with the Joneses, directing all earned money into buying the next thing and the next thing. When we direct our money into these purchases as opposed to wealth-building activities, we are never going to get ahead and more importantly, we're never going to feel financially well.

When I started to focus on financial wellness rather than wealth, things started to change massively. Being in control of money, being stable and building financial security for the future are the most empowering things anyone can do for themselves. When you do those things, it gives you solid financial foundations to then later build wealth for yourself, your family and your community.

References

Kiyosaki, R. T. (2000). *Rich Dad, Poor Dad.* Warner Books. ◈

DISRUPTING WEALTH MANAGEMENT

with Charlotte Ransom

Charlotte Ransom
NETWEALTH.COM

CHARLOTTE RANSOM *is
co-founder and CEO of wealth
manager Netwealth. Having
started her career at J.P. Morgan,
she spent 20 years at Goldman
Sachs, serving as one of the few
female partners for 10 years.*

> "
>
> The whole approach to the delivery of investing needs to evolve and I believe both women and men would benefit.

Charlotte holds the CISI Private Client Investment Advice and Management qualification and has been recognised by PAM as one *of the 50 Most Influential in 2019, 2020, and 2021 and awarded Wealth Manager of the Year and Woman of the Year, in 2019.*

How and when did you get started with investing? Tell us about the first investment you made.

When British Gas floated in 1986, its Tell Sid advertising campaign gave it one of the highest profiles of any privatisation. I was among those who got involved in investing for the first time. It was a fun way to begin the journey – I only bought a small amount but it piqued my interest, which was helped by the fact there were substantial gains!

What is your best, favourite or most worthwhile investment?

My favourite and most worthwhile investment has been launching Netwealth in 2016. I founded the company due to my frustration with traditional wealth managers who were not embracing new technology to improve client outcomes. We built proprietary technology that we combined with all the good bits of a traditional service. My life and my family's lives have been transformed by having our money centralised at Netwealth. And there is nothing better than going to work each day knowing that you are improving other investors' lives by providing a much-needed modern discretionary wealth management service.

What do you think the biggest barrier is for women investing?

Finance has always been an inherently male business. When I went into investment banking in the late 80s, I was one of a tiny percentage of women and it didn't change that dramatically over the next 25 years. Investing has tended to be considered a man's domain and, as a result, the language, service model, and staffing all reflect that. I am always coming across women who have been alienated from the process by being patronised and not feeling as though they are speaking to someone they trust.

What would you change to encourage more women to invest their money?

This is work in progress, but the whole approach to, and delivery of, investing needs to evolve and I believe both women and men would benefit. We can do so much more to make this critical topic more accessible and bring it higher up people's to-do lists. There is a real problem across the country in terms of lack of engagement and understanding about personal finance and investment.

What are you doing to encourage more equality in finance and investing?

As the CEO of a wealth management business I am very focused on achieving a diverse workforce as well as a diverse client base. My biggest success to date is that almost half our clients are female which is dramatically different from the norm of below 25%.

Do you think women have traits which give them an edge in investing? What trait(s) do you consider to be the secret weapon?

Women take a different approach to investing from men. They are typically more focused on achieving goals than seeking outright returns which gives them a more defined horizon and risk tolerance. They are often considered better investors since they tend not to try to time the market, and instead remain invested – this helps reduce friction costs and avoids the crystallisation of potential losses. I think there is room for both approaches.

Useful
Resources

FOUR

INSPIRATIONAL
INVESTING

Join the conversation on Facebook or Telegram:

f www.facebook.com/groups/inspirationalinvesting

✈ t.me/inspirationalinvesting

Connect • Inspire • Learn

RESOURCES DIRECTORY

The following pages include some useful resources to help with your investing journey:

Reading list

*_Own It!_ | Iona Bain

The Money Revolution: Easy Ways to Manage Your Finances in a Digital World | Anne Boden

How to Streamline Your Finances | Emillie Bellet

The Little Book of Common Sense Investing | John Bogle

The Richest Man in Babylon | George S. Clason

The Simple Path to Wealth | J.L. Collins

How to Own the World | Andrew Craig

*_The Laws of Wealth_ | Daniel Crosby

The Essays of Warren Buffet | Lawrence A. Cunningham

*_The Investment Trusts Handbook 2022_ | Jonathan Davis (free ebook available)

Winning the Losers Game | Charles D. Ellis

The Intelligent Investor | Benjamin Graham

*_The Psychology of Money_ | Morgan Housel

Rich Dad Poor Dad | Robert Kiyosaki

One up on Wall Street | Peter Lynch

* *The Meaningful Money Handbook* | Pete Matthew

Style and Substance: A Guide for Women Who Want to Win at Work | Helena Morrissey

I Will Teach you to be Rich | Ramit Sethi

Fooled by Randomness | Naseem Nicholas Taleb

Money: A User's Guide | Laura Whately

*Title available from Harriman House: Use Code: INSPIRATIONAL30 for a 30% discount

Podcasts

AJ Bell Money & Markets

Free and figuring it out – Money Special Ep 122–127

Interactive Investor

InvestED

Money Clinic with Claer Barrett

MoneyTalk Radio Finance Podcasts

The ii Family Money Show

The Money To The Masses Podcast

The MoneyWeek Podcast

The Wallet

Social media

Baillie Gifford | @BaillieGifford

Iona Bain | 🐦 @IonaYoungMoney 📷 @IonaJBain

Claer Barrett | 🐦 📷 @ClaerB @financialtimes

Rosie Carr | 🐦 @CarrRosie 🐦 @IChronicle 📷 @investorschronicle

Claire Dwyer | 🐦 @ClaireDwyer_

Kalpana Fitzpatrick | 🐦 📷 @KalpanaFitz 📷 themoneyedit_ 🐦 @MoneyEdit

Selina Flavius | 📷 @BlackGirlFinanceUK

Vivi Friedgut | 🐦 📷 @ViviFriedgut @Blackbullion

Prerna Khemlani | 📷 @ThisGirlInvests

Holly Mackay | 🐦 📷 @HollyAMackay @Boringmoney_hq

Helena Morrissey | 📷 @HelenaMorrissey 🐦 @MorrisseyHelena

Investors Chronicle | 🐦 @Ichronicle

Master Investor | 🐦 @MasterInvestor

Rebecca O'Connor | 🐦 @rebeccaoco

Laura Pomfret | 📷 @Financielle 🐦 @TheFinancielle

Scottish Widows | 🐦 @ScottishWidows

Amanda Taylor | 🐦 @Amandainvests 🐦 📷 @Investologyorg

Websites

30 Percent Club | 30percentclub.org

Baillie Gifford | bailliegifford.com

BlackBullion | www.blackbullion.com

Black Girl Finance | blackgirlfinance.co.uk

Boring money | boringmoney.co.uk

Citywire | citywire.co.uk

FCA | fca.org.uk

Fidelity | fidelity.co.uk

Financielle | financielle.co.uk

Finimize | finimize.com

FT | ft.com

FT Financial Literacy & Inclusion Campaign | ftflic.com

Good With Money | good-with-money.com

Harriman House | harriman-house.com

Investology | investology.org

Investors Chronicle | investorschronicle.co.uk

Interactive Investor | ii.co.uk

International Women's Day | internationalwomensday.com

Ladies Finance Club UK | ladiesfinanceclub.com

Master Investor | masterinvestor.co.uk

MoneyWeek | moneyweek.com

Morningstar | morningstar.co.uk

Scottish Widows | scottishwidows.co.uk

ShareTalk | share-talk.com

The Association of Investment Companies | theaic.co.uk

The Dura Society | thedurasociety.com

The Money Edit | themoneyedit.com

This Girl Invests | thisgirlinvests.co.uk

The UK Individual Shareholders' Society | sharesoc.org

Trustnet | trustnet.com

Young Money Blog | youngmoneyblog.co.uk

Platforms

A.J. Bell | ajbell.co.uk

Fidelity International | fidelity.co.uk

Hargreaves Lansdown | hl.co.uk

Interactive Investor | ii.co.uk

Vanguard | vanguardinvestor.co.uk

Events

Master Investor Show | 19th March 2022 / 18th March 2023 | Master InvestorShow.co.uk (*Use code: HARRIMAN for a free ticket*)

London Investor show | 28th October 2022 | londoninvestorshow.com

UK Investor Show | 21st May 2022 | ukinvestorshow.com

Research / Insights

London Stock Exchange | londonstockexchange.com

Edison Investment Research | edisongroup.com

QuotedData | quoteddata.com

London South East | lse.co.uk

A-Z OF INVESTING

Active management: when you invest in an actively managed fund, a professional fund manager will choose which investments to hold in the fund. The manager's aim is to deliver a performance that beats the fund's stated benchmark or index and they will actively buy, hold and sell investments to try to achieve this goal.

AIM: Alternative Investment Market (AIM) is a sub-market of the London Stock Exchange. There is no minimum size the company needs to be to list on AIM and they also don't require a trading record, which means many of the companies which join the market have only been around for a short period of time.

Asset allocation: asset allocation is deciding what proportion of a portfolio should be made up from different investments (such as equities, bonds or funds), markets, and sectors, taking into account the risk involved with each one.

Bear market: a bear market is a prolonged period of falling stock prices, usually marked by a decline of 20% or more. A market in which prices decline sharply against a background of widespread pessimism, growing unemployment or business recession.

Bid-offer spread: the *bid* refers to the price the market is willing to pay you if you want to sell your shares, whereas the *offer* is the price the market will sell you shares if you wish to buy them. The gap between the two prices is known as the *spread*. For shares that trade very frequently, this difference is likely to be quite narrow.

Bond: a bond is a loan issued by a corporation or government where they promise to repay the full amount on a specific date in the future, while also paying interest to the investor. Some bonds are structured in such a way that they make regular interest payments at a specific rate and over a specific period. Some bonds have interest rates that change over time.

Bull market: any market in which prices are advancing in an upward trend. In general, someone is bullish if they believe the value of a security or market will rise.

Capital gain: the difference between the price you pay for an investment and its selling price, when the difference is positive.

Commodities: wheat, livestock, oil, gold and sugar are all types of commodities. They are raw materials that are used to create a range of consumer products. Commodity investors study the markets for these products with the aim of predicting how prices will change in the future. Historically, prices of commodities have been very volatile, responding quickly to changes in the political and economic environment.

Compound interest: compounding is all about earning interest on your interest (or returns on your returns), rather than just on the original money you invested. The power of compounding can have a huge effect on your investment returns. If you don't make withdrawals and instead let your returns mount up over time, the knock-on effect can be substantial.

Diversification: the process of owning different investments that perform well in different market conditions. The aim is to reduce the effects of volatility (market ups and downs) on the portfolio, while boosting the potential for increased returns.

Dividends: dividends are payments made by companies to their shareholders out of their profits or reserves. They are not guaranteed. Investors can either take dividends as a cash payout, or reinvest them to boost the potential for growth over time.

ETF: an Exchange-Traded Fund (ETF) is a type of fund that tracks an index or market such as the FTSE 100 or S&P 500. ETFs are traded in the same way as individual shares, which means they can be bought and sold on the stock market. The share price changes throughout the day, depending on market movements.

Equities: shares issued by a company. A holding in a company gives the holder the entitlement to dividend payments and voting rights.

FTSE, FTSE 100: FTSE is an acronym for the Financial Times Stock Exchange. Today, the FTSE manages lists of companies – known as *indices* – trading on the London Stock Exchange to show how they're performing.

Fund: a pool of money from a group of investors that is managed by an investment manager. The investment manager takes the money and invests it in a wide range of assets such as equities and bonds. Unit trusts and open-ended investment companies are types of fund.

Growth investing: an investment strategy that focuses on stocks of companies and stock funds where earnings are growing rapidly and are expected to continue growing.

Investment strategy: a set of rules, behaviours or procedures designed to guide an investor's selection of a portfolio and meet their goals.

IPO: an Initial Public Offering (IPO) occurs when a business comes to the market for the first time and sells shares to the public just before they become available on a recognised stock exchange.

ISA: an Individual Savings Account (ISA), is a scheme allowing individuals to hold cash, shares, and unit trusts free of tax on dividends, interest, and capital gains.

Liquidity: how quickly and easily you're able to access money from your investment. The more shares a company has listed on the stock market, the more liquid the shares are, in theory.

Market capitalisation: (or market cap) refers to the market value of a company. It's calculated by multiplying the number of a company's shares by the price per share.

Open-ended investment companies (OEIC): a type of fund that is able to invest in other companies with an ability to constantly adjust its investment criteria and size, hence it is *open ended*.

Passive funds: the opposite of active funds, and also known as index trackers or tracker funds. Passive funds will buy all, or the majority, of the assets in a particular market – which in turn means the passive fund will closely mirror the performance of that index.

Portfolio: a collection of investments owned by one organisation or individual. These investments are managed collectively, with specific investment goals in mind.

Price-to-earnings ratio (P/E): a valuation measure that shows how much investors are paying for a particular company's earning power. It is calculated by taking the company's share price and dividing it by the earnings per share.

Risk attitude: all investments carry some degree of risk – the chance you will lose your capital. Traditionally, the greater the risk you take with your money, the greater the potential reward.

SIPP: a Self-Invested Personal Pension (SIPP) is a pension plan that enables the holder to choose and manage the investments made.

Stock market: a place where stocks and shares are bought and sold, for instance the London Stock Exchange.

Stocks, shares: these two terms are often used interchangeably. A stock is a share in a company. A company can separate its stock into a number of shares. Investors generally aim to buy them at one price and sell once the value has increased. Stockholders or shareholders usually receive dividends once or twice a year, which are paid from the company's profits.

Unit trusts: a collective investment that holds assets and passes the profits from the underlying assets/investments to the owners of those units, as opposed to reinvesting them in the fund.

PARTNERS

Independent Global Investment Managers

Baillie Gifford is privately and wholly owned by its partners. This is the crucial underpinning of our approach: we have no short-term commercial imperatives and no outside shareholders to distract us. We can simply do what's right for clients, and that's what has sustained our business since 1908.

We are the largest manager of investment trusts in the UK with a range of thirteen trusts. We have an extensive range of OEIC sub-funds and manage investments globally for pension funds, institutions and charities.

Some see the collective failure of active management as an argument to embrace passive. We see it as an opportunity to redefine our original purpose of deploying clients' capital into tangible, returns generating activities. And we believe that redefinition is 'actual investment'.

Actual investment is not easy in our world of 24-hour news, where complexity and noise is confused with rational judgement. It requires the resolve to focus only on what really matters, to think independently and to maintain a long-term perspective. It requires a willingness to be different, to accept uncertainty and the possibility of being wrong.

Most of all, it requires a rejection of the now conventional wisdom that has led our industry astray: investment management is not about processing power, trading and speed. It is about imagination and creativity, and working constructively on behalf of our clients with inspiring individuals and companies who have greater ideas than our own.

The best investment ideas spring from thinking about future possibilities, not short-term probabilities. Our research covers the globe and we set no barriers to the imagination of our investors, encouraging fresh perspectives and the use of diverse sources of information.

We believe our approach to investing not only best delivers good outcomes for clients, but it also helps to develop great companies that provide for the needs and wants of people, thereby benefiting society as a whole. Investing responsibly for the long term is not counter to outperforming for clients, it's intrinsic to it.

The value of a stock market investment and any income from it can fall as well as rise and investors may not get back the amount invested. Your capital is at risk. Baillie Gifford & Co Limited is authorised and regulated by the Financial Conduct Authority.

About Scottish Widows

Scottish Widows was founded in 1815 and has since established a proud history of helping customers plan and protect their financial futures.

Today, Scottish Widows has almost six million customers and offers a product range including individual and workplace pensions, annuities, mortgages, savings and investments, life insurance and critical illness cover. Their aim is to help customers plan for a secure financial future.

It is therefore no surprise that Scottish Widows currently sits as one of the most recognised and trusted brands in the Life Pensions & Investments market.* The brand's credentials continue to grow having gained a prestigious Financial Adviser 5 Star rating across Life Insurance and Pensions, and Investments categories, as well as the Editor's Achievement Award for 30 years' consistent service.

Since 1986, the brand has become synonymous with its iconic 'living logo', the Scottish Widow, who has featured in advertising for over 30 years. 'Taking on your Future Together' is the latest advert to feature the Scottish Widow and this commitment underpins everything we do – from delivering expertise, guidance and insight to providing products to help people plan for their future.

Scottish Widows is committed to helping people across the UK prepare for the future. The brand has a longstanding research program focused on UK financial planning attitudes, regular sponsorship of Pension Awareness Day and a suite of 'Pension Basics' films covering a wide range of scenarios to help get people thinking about their future plans.

The company headquarters remains in Edinburgh, the city in which it was established, and in 2009 Scottish Widows became part of the UK's largest financial group, the Lloyds Banking Group.

For more information on Scottish Widows visit **www.scottish widows.co.uk**

* Prompted Awareness rank: 1, Trust (Character) rank: 1(=), Trust (Competence): 3(=). IPSOS, December 2020.